The Trouble
with You
Innerleckchuls

Marion
Montgomery

All inquiries should be addressed to:
Christendom College Press, Front Royal, VA 22630.

Sections *i* and *ii* were originally published in *Studies in the Literary Imagination*, Vol. XX, No. 2, Fall 1987.

For Gerhart Niemeyer

Who, seeing "the desert in the garden the garden in the desert of drouth," teaches us the joy of intellectual husbandry.

i

A colleague of mine, one particularly skilled in textual analysis and structural and symbolic dimensions of modern literature, remarked to me that he finds Flannery O'Connor "anti-intellectual" in her fiction, a remark which at first took me very much by surprise. On reflection, though, one sees how such an impression is possible, particularly insofar as one responds to the surface presences of Miss O'Connor's sophisticated or pseudo-sophisticated characters, for instance to Julian in "Everything That Rises Must Converge." Then there are her own remarks that don't seem to help her case, especially informal ones such as her saying to a correspondent, "Me and Enoch are living in the woods in Connecticut with the Robert Fitzgeralds. Enoch don't care so much for New York."[1] She seems rather to be siding with Enoch than satirizing his attitude toward that sophisticated world whose capital in this country is conceded to be New York City. Why would she, even in fun, associate herself with Enoch? It seems unseemly. And when one adds to her playful remarks the very deliberate castigation of the sophisticated Easterner, one might indeed begin to suspect her of being anti-intellectual. The critics of New York City, she says in "The Regional Writer," are an "unreliable lot, as incapable now as on the day they were born of interpreting Southern literature to the world."[2] It is as if such a critic is victim of an arrested

---

[1]Flannery O'Connor, "To Robie Macauley," 1950, *The Habit of Being*, ed. Sally Fitzgerald (New York: Farrar, Straus, and Giroux, 1979), p. 21.

[2]*Mystery and Manners* (New York: Farrar, Straus, and Giroux), p. 55.

intellectualism the obverse of Enoch's arrested wise blood. As for "the Northern reader," in speaking of the grotesque in modern fiction she says that reader is going to take anything that comes out of the South as grotesque, "unless it is grotesque, in which case it is going to be called realistic."[3]

What one begins to suspect, especially in the context from which such statements are taken, is that Flannery O'Connor is objecting to a provincialism, a term traditionally reserved for application to the South and to Southerners. Perhaps she isn't so much anti-intellectual as Southern chauvinist? But then, her objection is that the New York critic is incapable of interpreting to "the world," which suggests that she has a larger arena in mind than her local listeners. Aha! Then how is one to account for her presentation of Hulga, a Ph.D. learned in French Existentialism? Hardly a flattering presentation of that European "world view." Doesn't Hulga suggest with more certainty that in "Good Country People" Miss O'Connor reveals herself both skeptical about the intellectual in the larger world and, at best, amused by the ignorance of her Southern "good" country people? Is she an elitist of some sort, reserving a very limited and withdrawn arena to herself?

Well, no. She isn't making fun of Enoch or of Hulga's mama, Mrs. Hopewell, in quite the way this question suggests. There is a level of sympathy that undercuts caricature, though some of her critics have taken her "good country people" at that level only. In Hulga's case (she was named Joy Hopewell), it is Hulga who rather bitterly ridicules country people, and in a very sophisticated way. The name *Joy Hopewell* (which a Hawthorne might have been tempted to use for its allegorical suggestiveness) is Hulga's by inheritance out of a residual piety in her mother; the piety lingers long after its spiritual roots have decayed in her mother's community. That decay, we note in passing here, is

---

[3]"Some Aspects of the Grotesque in Southern Fiction," *Mystery and Manners*, p. 40.

precisely out of a decay of the intellect, a point Hulga does not miss. Indeed, that is the key to what is for Hulga a decidedly Nominalistic irony which she plays out. Her mother thinks that names name things, and so if one names a thing right, its thingness comes to reside the more fully in the name itself. Not, of course, that Mrs. Hopewell thinks in so explicit a way. That is why one says it is residual in her, lost below the level of deliberate intellect, as meaning tends to become lost when words are automatic to us.

Hulga, recognizing the circumstances of mind in the world immediately about her, takes perverse delight in changing her name from *Joy* to *Hulga*. She is given to an intellectual conjuring unlike her mother's vapid conjuring of the good and virtuous, but with a pride of intellect she has acquired through her "education." Her mother's conjuring of good to Hulga, by supplying "Joy" to "Hopewell," still supposes the source of a possible Joy in Hope to lie outside herself. Names, for her, would signify realities if she were to think about it, the kind of country wisdom Miss O'Connor herself is very sympathetic to. On the other hand, Hulga's conjuring is of quite another sort. Given her "philosophical" position, she is decidedly Nominalist, but of a very modern breed of Nominalism, the Sartrean Existentialist kind. The source from which the signifier, the word, holds its authority is her own mind only. Her chosen name, Hulga, is an arbitrary choice, dictated by its ugliness as sound. What she intends is to fill that ugliness with her own self-made ugliness, ugliness being as acceptable to her as beauty since neither has legitimate reference to any reality separate from her own will. In addition (and in contradiction to her own position), there is the added fillip: the name irritates her mother. The only advantage to her is that of irony, not even fully perceived by Mrs. Hopewell as irony but only as unnatural disobedience. Which indeed it is, for Flannery O'Connor no less than for Mrs. Hopewell.

Hulga, in this respect, has come to the same conclusion the Misfit does, though he sees more clearly than she. Or rather, whereas the Misfit presents alternatives between which he cannot resolutely choose, Hulga has made her arbitrary choice. Having decided that Christ was not what he is reported to be, Hulga finds "No pleasure but meanness," and rather little of that. At most, she is petty. It appears, in the course of the story, that Hulga's self-ugliness as a rejection of all existence save what existence she wills runs head-long into a fundamental reality, namely that ugliness has an existence independent of her own making, of which indeed her making is but a dependent sub-species. That is the shocking recognition, through the Bible salesman who was born believing in absolute ugliness — in nothingness. He required no doctorate in philosophy to arrive at that position. He too operates in a Nominalist way, to his own pleasure, but in a way opposite Hulga's: he cultivates to his own advantage the "beautiful" and the "good," or what appears to be the beautiful and good to decayed intellects such as Mrs. Hopewell's. By Nominalistic acts he makes himself a "good country" person to people who comfortably think of themselves as such. His is the more subtle, the more sophisticated irony, though it has little audience. For Hulgas in rural Georgia are relatively rare.

Hulga, we must remember, is the story's protagonist; and she comes to a vision beyond intellectual illusions, which is to say that in such a dramatization of mind's encounter with inevitable reality the maker of that drama, Flannery O'Connor, reveals herself to be very much what she said she was, a "hillbilly Thomist." The world she addresses is not a local one. Neither is it that provincial world of the intellect disengaged from reality, the world which seems the only one to her "New York critics." As she remarks to "A" in a letter, "My audience are the people who think God is dead. At least these are the people I am conscious of writing for."[4] As for a Mrs. Hopewell — and Mrs. Hopewells are not so legion as are Miss O'Connor's chosen audience —

---

[4]"To 'A.'," 2 August 1955, *The Habit of Being*, p. 92.

though she has only a residual emotional relation to the existence of God, the one position she would never say in words is that God is dead. She may act intellectually as if He were, but it is not shibboleth or residual thought for her as for Miss O'Connor's audience. But if faith in Mrs. Hopewell has been reduced to an emotional residue by a decay of intellect, residual faith has been deliberately rooted out by Hulga through intellect itself. In making this point to "A," Miss O'Connor remarks that Hulga's "fine education has got rid of [faith] for her." The real problem is that "purity has been overridden by *pride* of intellect," not by intellect (my italics).⁵

It is the same circumstance involved in Haze Motes's assault upon the world, reflected in his fierce insistence that he is clean, his own purity established by the fierce insistence. But Haze, too, is Nominalist, in one part of his being. Onnie Jay Holy (John Holy, a "theologian" capable of Pig Latin but not of St. Thomas's Latin) sees a wonderful opportunity for a con-game using Haze's idea for "a new jesus." He wants to join forces with Haze. He wants to discover and display such a "new jesus," using Haze's passionate violence of words, but Haze rebuffs him: there is "no such thing as a new jesus." That is just "a way to say something," the words having no anchor in nature, in a reality. They are only an irritating presence in Haze's mind. Onnie Jay responds with bitter disappointment: "That's just the trouble with you innerleckchuls. . . . you don't never have nothing to show for what you're saying." Considering Haze's intellectual position at the time, Onnie Jay is exactly right, though he is disappointed for the wrong reasons. Haze will be shocked to discover him right when Enoch Emory presents him with that "new jesus" which corresponds with a disturbing literalness to Haze's detailed description of the new jesus: Haze's Church Without Christ, he has said, needs a new jesus "that's all man, without blood to waste, and it needs one that don't look like any man so you'll look

---

⁵"To 'A.'," 24 August 1956, *The Habit of Being*, pp. 170-171.

at him." When Enoch delivers the stolen mummy, Haze's Nominalist words turn against him, bludgeoning him with a "something" that exactly fits his words.

Flannery O'Connor herself believes, with Onnie Jay, that Haze shows in his intellectual journey up to this point "what is wrong with you innerleckchuls," a phrase she aims more broadly than just at Haze. For Haze exhibits the weakness of intellect gone astray, of intellect overpowered by pride. Such an intellect is quite content to find its rest in "a way of saying something," divorcing that way from an encompassing reality. That is the comfortable position Miss O'Connor's elected audience would maintain, and she is unwilling to leave them comfortable. She takes a mischievous delight in suggesting that one may hold Nietzsche's nihilistic ideas about the world without having been given "what passes for an education in this day and time," the sort of "formal" education she admits she shares with the intellectual community. To this remark, in a letter to Ben Griffith, she adds, "I am not deceived by it."[6] Through a character like Haze, then, she says to her audience what the Bible salesman says directly to Hulga: "You ain't so smart."

The point she is making in such fiction she speaks of rather more directly in her letters and essays. She believes that our age, and especially those of us in the sophisticated intellectual community, has been "brought up under many forms of false intellectual discipline such as 19th-century mechanism. . . ."[7] She has a great deal to say about false "innerleckchuls," but it is the *false* that concerns her, not the *intellectual*, to which she is firmly committed. To see just what she means by the *false* requires an analysis deeper and broader than her fiction alone, an analysis moving in directions suggested by her considerable readings in Western intellectual history and her comments in the light of that reading. Thus, to enlarge the question of modern

---

[6]"To Ben Griffith," 13 February 1954, *The Habit of Being*, p. 68.
[7]"To 'A.'," 6 September 1955, *The Habit of Being*, p. 100.

"intellectualism" is to discover what she means by her repeated claim that as an imaginative writer she is committed to reason. She is a "realist of distances" in her own vision, while as artist she is very much insistent that "In art reason goes wherever the imagination goes. We have reduced the uses of reason terribly. You say a thing is reasonable and people think you mean it is safe. What's reasonable is seldom safe and always exciting."[8] If we discover what she means by our world's having "reduced the uses of reason terribly," we will begin to understand why she can say of such "innerleckchuls" as Haze Motes, "Of course, I think of Haze Motes as a kind of saint."[9] We shall rather certainly begin to appreciate her in her own person, as distinct from her art, as a most remarkable intellectual, a "hillbilly Thomist." We begin our concern with an address to Manicheanism in the modern mind, that mind she deliberately elects as audience. More specifically, we shall approach her repeated use of "Manichean" by first considering what I take to be a more inclusive term, *modern gnosticism*. She encountered that term in her reading, but it has been more widely used in philosophy and theology in pursuit of the problem of "modernism" since her death in 1964.

---

[8]Betsy Lockridge, "An Afternoon with Flannery O'Connor," *Atlanta Journal-Constitution*, 1 November 1959.

[9]"To Ben Griffith," 9 July 1955, *The Habit of Being*, p. 89.

ii

Since the work of such scholars as Eric Voegelin, Hans Jonas, Gerhart Niemeyer, and many others, we encounter the term *secular* or *modern gnosticism* at every turn. It is an attempt to characterize an address to creation by the intellect on the intellect's sole authority — an address engaging not only the world of nature but that of human nature and social, political, and religious institutions as well. The term *gnostic* is various in its uses, ancient and modern, depending upon the limited application of the moment, so that I ought to make my own understanding of it as clear as I may. But here I intend only to characterize a climate of thought rather than attempt an inclusive analysis; that thought is sufficiently general among us to be recognized by abbreviated description. Concerning one of its species, Flannery O'Connor remarks, "if you live today you breathe in nihilism. In or out of the Church, it's the gas you breathe."[1] If the constituent elements of modern gnosticism are several, a most various gas in this air that we all breathe, there is the additional complexity of a relative thickness or thinness of those constituents wherever we variously gather, two or three of us, to breathe. The degree and variety of its elements, however, are so pervasive as to make the intellectual atmosphere almost palpable, a climate of thought hovering over us like the smog over a California city. None of us entirely escape it, our own breathing affected to the extent that, in turn, few of us avoid contributing additionally to the pollution.

---

[1]"To 'A.'," 28 August 1955, *The Habit of Being*, p. 97.

In general we may say that gnosticism, by intellectual fiat, reduces "matter" or "body" or "nature" or "creation" — terms with kindred meanings and intent but separate nuances. This attitude toward existence has a passive presence in all of us; by the illusion that by not willing to act against it we are at least neutral, we conclude ourselves not party to the deconstructions of creation. In its virulent stage, which infects our passive attitude, modern gnosticism intends to reduce existence by separating mind or spirit from all else through the active, violent power of its own thought, whose immediate instrument, tailored to the given occasion, is words. In a vocabulary made popular through phenomenology and psychology, and in the philosophies that grow out of those recent concentrations of mind upon existence, gnostic thought separates consciousness from the content of consciousness. It separates "subject" from "object." It is a movement of mind against existence which Flannery O'Connor has specifically in mind when she remarks that, when the writer spurns a religious view of existence, he engages in separations inimical to art: "Judgment will be separated from vision, nature from grace, and reason from imagination."[2] She knows better than most of us that not only are writers self-endangered through such deliberate or accidental separations, but the health of any intellectual community is put at spiritual risk. And she knows the symptoms as well as the inevitable effects.

When such maneuvers against existence are deliberate by the mind, or even when only passively acceded to by mind, the effect is a presumption that mind is elevated over existence; consciousness transcends all that is not mind itself. But, reason itself must tell us, the agency in this transcendent action is finite consciousness; when consciousness thereby assumes itself absolute over being (including its own, as with Hulga) it becomes entangled in a contradiction. The finite as absolute is a self-

---

[2]"Catholic Novelists and Their Readers," *Mystery and Manners*, p. 184.

preparation for a disastrous encounter with reality, as when Hulga encounters the Bible salesman or Haze the mummy. Nevertheless, this is the journey of mind through which it arrives at a position Miss O'Connor describes in speaking of modern alienation as a literary theme. The modern hero can go anywhere but belongs nowhere: "The borders of his country are the sides of his skull."[3] Against such pretense of the heroic, sprung out of modern gnosticism, she poses her pathetic Julian in "Everything That Rises Must Converge." Julian is at last forced to concede himself citizen of a world beyond his skull, despite his attempt to maintain his isolation. He spends most of his time within an "inner compartment. . . . This was a kind of mental bubble in which he established himself when he could not bear to be a part of what was going on around him. From it he could see out and judge but in it he was safe from any kind of penetration from without." His condition is that of an intellectual AIDS, self-induced.

The consequence of such intellectual isolation from existence — not only in respect to our judgment of it from an orthodox faith about existence such as Miss O'Connor's but in relation to the realities of our experience of the world even at a secular level — is necessarily destructive of consciousness. That is, man in his natural no less than in his supernatural dimension is reduced by presumption. What is lost in the reduction is a recognition of potential being. Concerned to recover the largeness of one's being, one may be content to consider a potential fullness of being only within the natural limitations of existence, a limit which when it is the artist's may lead him to write "a great tragic naturalism," Miss O'Connor says, "for by his responsibility to the things he sees, he may transcend the limitations of his narrow vision." In other words, one may reject the supernatural but go beyond the limits of his own skull in a

---

[3]"The Catholic Writer in the Protestant South," *Mystery and Manners*, p. 200.

consent to the existence of objects, of a world outside a private mind. Or one may address that potential fullness in relation to the natural world as subsumed by the transcendent — become a "realist of distances." But through either act of faith, a partial or fuller movement out of the bubble of the self, one discovers reality beyond himself: he admits that he is a creature among creatures and is stirred on the way to becoming himself.

In the scholastic phrase, he is *homo viator* — man on-the-way, a description of man's being most dangerous to deny, even if one is willing to assert only the most secular level of existence. Miss O'Connor, writing in and to a secular age whose intellectual community is dominated by gnostic power, makes her vision of our age's emptiness by dramatizing characters who attempt to elevate and enlarge the self over creation, at the expense of insistent reality.   In doing so, they discover that they have reduced themselves from their given potential, since reality with ruthlessness crashes in upon the self they have vacuumized. Some of her protagonists — Haze Motes and Young Tarwater, for instance — are discovered "on their way" at literal levels, resolutely insisting on movement in a landscape but toward vague ends, hoping they will recognize those ends when reached. Haze is in pursuit of "a place that is no place," his rat-colored Essex the closest approximation he can come to — a machine of mind, operated by his will but lifeless; that is, without a significant being except for his will's presence. More often, her protagonist is intent on controlling the bit of local world to which he (or rather *she* more appropriately) holds legal, secular title. This protagonist establishes an arena within which she is the only absolute, though struggling against sorry specimens of humanity and a recalcitrant nature to maintain an absolute rule over being. The Georgia farm world at a particular juncture of history (post-World War II) is most amenable in its social and natural dimensions for these fictional purposes, and one need only recall Mrs. Lucynell Crater in "The Life You Save May Be Your Own," Mrs. May in "Greenleaf," Mrs. Cope in "A Circle of Fire," Mrs.

Turpin in "Revelation" to realize the clever uses Miss O'Connor makes of the local.

The willed separation of consciousness from existence, in the interest of the self as absolute — whether practiced by the ancient Gnostic heretic or by his secular descendent — is doomed in Flannery O'Connor's view, a conviction her stories dramatize. Her protagonists fail again and again, but in such a way that hope is restored. For, although she is too good an artist to conclude a story's actions with an assured rescue of her protagonist, she does restore the fallen character to a contingency. Where initially he is rather moving toward nihilistic oblivion, in the end another possibility is allowed. Thus her character is restored to the country in which hope is possible, though he is neither certainly damned nor saved. It is in respect to the denouement that restores spiritual contingency that her work is properly called comedy in Dante's sense, though it is laced throughout with a comedy in the popular sense. (That popular comedy sometimes becomes slapstick, as in Enoch Emory's interview with Gonga, the gorilla, who extends "the first hand that had been extended to Enoch since he had come to the city.")

Her characters, both despite themselves and because of themselves, are returned to a contingency of their being by the intrusion of a presence into their established arenas, or by an arrest of their noplace (Haze's auto) whereby it becomes a very specific place. Indeed, the generalization one comes to is that in her fiction the antagonist is always an intrusive grace, the protagonist being an agent intent upon proving himself sufficient by will through certain actions that exile being. She makes the point in a letter to "A": "All my stories are about the action of grace on a character who is not very willing to support it, but most people think of these stories as hard, hopeless, brutal, etc."[4] In short, her fiction's common theme is the devastating effect of

---

[4]"To 'A.'," 4 April 1958, *The Habit of Being*, p. 275.

mercy upon seemingly backwoods gnostics. Hope is left implicit in the final shambles, in that the destruction is a necessary prelude to the possibility of a substantial recovery of the protagonist's being.

It was mistakenly assumed when the stories first began to appear, and it continues to be, that she writes a very sophisticated kind of local color with sociological implications. But what interests her is the condition of the modern intellectual. That is the issue in this fiction, rather than representations of rural characters whose concrete historical presence misleads some "New York critics." The pole of grace on the one hand and of the finite gnostic mind on the other establish the intellectual ground within which the fiction's dramatic tension arcs, sputters into a climax, and then calms to a steady glow when the reality of existence — of being — reasserts itself with persuasive finality. Hence we discover that her protagonists are, in their spiritual state, reflections through art of the larger, geographically foreign (one might call it New Yorkish) intellectual community where gnosticism is dominant and from whence it trickles down through Atlanta (Taulkingham), even unto rural Georgia. She says this to be so and says it in plain enough language in letters and essays. But that her agents are reflections of that larger self-insured gnostic world is signalled as well by the disquiet with which her fiction was and is received in many otherwise sophisticated quarters.

The attempt to declare Haze Motes or the Misfit merely backwoods psychopaths, the sort of unfortunate, deprived creatures on the evening news for whom poverty programs and rehabilitation programs are designed, is only a momentary stay against confusion, against a shock of self-recognition. Her chosen audience doesn't remain safe, since the stories keep saying, shouting in an irresistible way, "you can't be poorer than dead" — dead spiritually and intellectually. And so her characters turn out to be, when examined by the full light of intellect, gnostics in hillbilly clothing, being presented to us by this self-declared "hillbilly Thomist." Beneath the fictional accidents of the local lurks the arresting and damning presence of the social and ideological thought that is predominant in deracinated sophisticates. Miss O'Connor suggests them excruciatingly inadequate at the intellectual level of man's encounter with existence precisely because of a deliberate, a self-imposed provincial understanding of their own minds and of the world. Her elected audience dawns slowly to her deft skewering of their ideas and arguments. What she reveals as their dominant weakness is a pride of intellect, and it is this pride that issues in an untenable provincialism more deadly than of having been born in the rural South. Little wonder, then, if some protest her to be anti-intellectual, when it can no longer be maintained that her fiction is local color used to satirize local yokels.

iii

The separation of the self from creation by an act of intellect results in a tortured alienation because creation has been fundamentally misunderstood in that willful act of mind. It is a misunderstanding which creation itself constantly reminds the alienated consciousness of. Reality's nagging reminder to the alienated, when not responded to directly and so openly engaged, leads the mind and spirit to be vulnerable to an inundating *angst*. In that state — a state of intellectual sloth — despair has its way with both mind and spirit; one is no longer open to the prospect of hope. With what sentimental languor has our age clasped *angst* to its bosom, only to wonder at last whether there is a bosom to which to clasp it. On this relation of sloth to the despair which our philosophy has attempted to make respectable by calling it *angst*, one should notice that both these conditions of spirit (sloth and the resulting despair) are more often signalled by intense and desperate activity than by a retreat into arrested inactivity. To recognize the spectacle accompanying sloth and the desperation of despair is to appreciate depths in the surface actions of a Haze Motes. He is caught up by despair into frenzied action, but at the end of *Wise Blood* he is restored to a state of hope. I say this, knowing that he seems to the modern mind to be listless and hopeless at the end. But it is only then that he has at last discovered the true end that has made him aimlessly agitated up to his last few days, the end which has at last drawn him beyond himself. He is, at the last, approaching the fullness of a rest desired all along through his "wise blood."

A failure to see this complexity in Haze Motes is to misread him, even at the merely psychological level. But not to see the spiritual nature of his condition prevents one's understanding what Miss O'Connor intends in saying that Haze is for her "a sort of saint." This failure, which I fear rather a common one, is evidence of the general intellectual and spiritual malaise that affects our age and against which Miss O'Connor resolutely sets herself, without compromising her art. For though we have taken some pleasure in describing ours as the Age of Alienation, it would be more accurate I think to call it the Age of Acedia. Those actions in the world which we associate with the "Puritan work ethic," which most of us think ourselves freed of, may even themselves be signs of intellectual acedia, the absence of spiritual magnanimity and joy in existence, and hence the actual reason they make one uncomfortable when confronted by those actions. One need only recall the confusions in Mrs. Turpin of "Revelation" on this point. These "Puritan" actions may be, as Mrs. Turpin discovers largely against her will, signals of a condition that must be engaged if a significant hope is to be restored in the spirit. For the true reality of our being cannot be hidden behind the signs we attempt to erect to hide ourselves, our activities in the world that keep us worldly. That is the devastating discovery Hawthorne's Young Goodman Brown makes about Puritan signs.

Here, then, I address *sloth* in its strict theological sense, not in its degenerate sense. And on this complex of the soul's journey to nothingness through *acedia*, mayhap accompanied by seemingly vigorous actions in the world, one has an excellent primer in Josef Pieper's *On Hope*.[1] Pieper's little book, a theological explication of the virtue of hope, is acutely perceptive, not only at the metaphysical level, but at the psychological levels of mind as well. As such, it is a good antidote to gnostic infections of intellect, the pathology of which we are examining. It is especially helpful since the psychological has

---

[1]Josef Pieper. *On Hope*, tr. Mary Frances McCarthy (San Francisco: Ignatius, 1986).

been presented so steadily in this century as the ultimate level of our understanding of mind. In showing a legitimate level to psychological knowledge without certifying it ultimate, *On Hope* provides a significant first step toward a recovery of intellectual complexity from the reductionist metaphors of Freudian and post-Freudian psychology. Let us prepare a way for Pieper's helpfulness to our concerns, then, by considering somewhat further this gnostic deconstruction of intellect that has made ours the Age of Acedia.

The ancient Gnostic, by an act of intellect, pries creation loose from its Creator and in the violence of that action casts creation toward outer darkness, as if thereby to rescue both God and the Gnostic's own spirit from evil. The rescue is his presumptuous anticipation, insofar as he believes that *gnosis* — a refined and secret knowledge — purifies spirit of the taint of creation. *Gnosis*, indeed, is a substitution made for the mystery of Christ's blood. By implication, the binding of spirit to the transcendent good through *gnosis* is effective whether God wills it or not. Thus for the Gnostic heretic, the Incarnation can have only a figurative meaning, lest even the word's etymology lure intellect dangerously to the world. Though Haze is no formal philosopher, he understands the point well enough when he struggles to reject any actual being, separate from his intellect, as the "new jesus." The phrase "new jesus" is just "a way to say something" which is no-thing. Lacking logical sophistry, Haze is struck with the problem any gnostic is stuck with: only through *somethingness* can *nothingness* even be suggested, which means that the gnostic's *nothingness* is always dependent upon a something of which he is not ultimately the cause and for which he cannot claim credit as creator.

Words, then, have an almost malevolent intent (seen from the gnostic point of view) in that they insist on some anchor in bodily anchored things, even ideas. Even at their most abstract, words are haunted by a seeming origin in concrete existence, in creation. The Incarnation, more than the Resurrection, is the dangerous event to gnosticism, since by intellect the gnostic believes he can perform his own resurrection, an intellectual act whereby he rises above existence. Against that view of mind's relation to creation, which she sees as present and dominant in our world, Flannery O'Connor says, in "Catholic Novelists and Their Readers," "Christ didn't redeem us by direct intellectual act, but became incarnate in human form."[2] The old Gnostic understands the contrary. In being created "in the image of God," his spiritual perfection requires an intellect purified of all creation save his own spirit as the image of God to be elevated untouched by the world's actuality. A part of this process is the purging of a word like *redeem* of its worldly aura, of its sense imagery — the *taking back*, the *buying back*. To *take* implies a use of force available to the intellect only by analogy to force in nature.

The rational, gnostic intellect must, therefore, cut itself off from an intrusion of the visionary, since the visionary is dependent upon bodily existence as the medium of vision. To the degree the severance is successful, however, the Gnostic spirit will find itself, not transported to beatitude as it desires, but isolated from both the world and from God. Thus in a signal act, long remembered, the most famous of the Gnostics castrated himself. Even so, he was not yet freed of the entangling world. Origen's "graduate assistants" conferred the epithet *chalkenteros* on him — "the worker with brazen bowels." Perhaps we may from that epithet conclude that the more firmly one struggles to reject creation (in this instance the procreative body) the more concrete — the more petrified — it becomes. It is, after all, on this rock of creation, with all its hidden fissures, that God builds his church.

A less homely figure for the point one finds in the opening of the *Divine Comedy*. Dante's pilgrim self, in attempting to escape the dark wood of the world, climbs anxiously toward the

---

[2]*Mystery and Manners*, p. 176.

sun he has just rediscovered. He is forced back into the world by
the Leopard, to a further encounter with the Wolf; these are
suitable creatures to represent the wily sensuousness of intellect
(Leopard) and ravenous predatory power in nature (Wolf),
though they are symbols otherwise read by critical allegorists.
The point suggested by the episode in the poem, however, is that
one suitably approaches the "sun" by enduring the world as
bathed by the "sun," a bathing so deep as to lie at the heart of the
matter of the world itself. One properly shuns a presumption of
rescue by engaging creation, even when that engagement
requires a descent back into darkness out of a moment of light.
Dante's great poem thereafter dramatizes the visionary journey
as necessarily using the gifts of our particular being in relation to
the particularity of creation; that is what his pilgrim, a creature in
a created world, learns.

For the Gnostic blinded in his direct pursuit of the sun, the
intellect is seen as most dangerously susceptible to emotion,
impulse, instinct and the like representation of the conditions of
our being human, because those intrusions upon pure thought
are seen as temporally anchored in space. They are anchored in
the body, which thus becomes antagonist. The Gnostic response
is to declare the necessity of a thing that is not a thing, "a way of
saying something," which only by the act of saying becomes a
something. Thus intellect, the Gnostic starting point, itself is
"embodied" as concept. The flaw here is that concept is not
actuality, but dependent upon an actuality; when addressed as if
actual, concept becomes an illusion. (We shall presently see this
flaw at the heart of the latest critical movement, Deconstruction.)
Thus for the gnostic mind, intellect becomes idol. The will by
gnosis asserts its God-like image, whether the willful mind be the
ancient Gnostic heretic or his secular descendant. Thus intellect
appears to become the whole man, the ideal limit of human
being, however troublesome the clinging residue of the body may
be. Rational intellect, through the grace of *gnosis*, rejects its
entrapment in "the world" as the action necessary if its spirit (or

its mind for the secularist) is to be saved. Complex existence is thus actively expunged from mind, the issues of which action very often are precise and elegant conceptual paradigms of being from which actual being has been removed to give a moment's comfort of gnostic consciousness. One discovers just such "images" of intellect, gnostic images, sometimes in poets (I have in mind Wallace Stevens and his limits of the imagination, his "necessary angel"); but more insistently one finds them in "poetic" programs such as Darwinism or Marxism or Freudianism or, most recently, Feminism. Having mentioned the ancient Gnostic's concern for the "soul," a clarification is here in order so that we may see affinities between the ancient and the secular gnostic. The old Gnostic distinguishes *pneuma* (spirit) from *psyche* (soul) in order that he may engage and exorcise what he takes to be his perverse "spiritual" attraction to existence. *Pneuma* (spirit) is to be rescued to beatitude against *psyche* (soul), for the *psyche* is of and in the world; it is a purchase upon his spirit made by a demiurge in nature. The *psyche*, then, is of the body, of the world, and is therefore the principal antagonist, the secret agent in him of a foreign governor of the world. He has been invaded and his spirit reduced from pristine.

Presently we shall suggest that this heresy is consequent upon the "psyche" misunderstood. We shall hold that what the Gnostic takes as foreign agent is rather, in the orthodox view, recognized as a gift of being in the soul — a mode of knowing which is companionable to the rational mode and which indeed opens the soul to the mystery of being. It is through this drawing into an openness to being that the soul moves toward beatitude, becomes truly "on-the-way." We shall be considering, then, that what the Gnostic calls *psyche* is a perversion of a commonly recognized faculty which the orthodox scholastic calls *intellectus*. Abiding that point, we observe here that the gnostic's operation of intellect attempts to remove or emaciate the *intellectus* in order to become beatifically transformed. There is a deliberate rejection of the complexity of existence, most specifically of a part of his own gift of being (the *intellectus*), and that accomplished, the rejection of creation in general, including his own body, follows. But this is a heresy both ancient and contemporary; one finds it within the visible Church, past and present; one finds it even more abundantly in our day in the secular world (Freudianism, for instance, is an active carrier of the confusion). What we now turn to is its manifestation impinging upon the soul from the secular world; let us consider further this *secular gnosticism*, the term with which we began our exploration.

iv

Eric Voegelin, in *Science, Politics and Gnosticism*, remarks that "Gnosis desires dominion over being." In that work, and in *From Enlightenment to Revolution* and *The Ecumenic Age*,[1] he explores the modern gnostic's various attempts upon creation, attempts through which the body of the world is to be "de-natured" as the means of controlling that which is not the self — actions nearly always declared done in the general name of Humanity. What Voegelin describes is a secular religion, one that intends the self-salvation of that abstraction Humanity. We have already seen that this same desire for dominion over being characterizes the ancient Gnostic as well. The significant shift, since the late medieval world, has been to a dominion by man established as his own God. The modern gnostic's separation from existence is the leverage he believes needed to restructure being at a fundamental level. The gauche attempt by the alchemist in the opening of the Renaissance was an attempt to seize at once by violence the citadel of being, and when the frontal assault on being collapsed, a more subtle program began, one through which "uncounted petty thefts" (in Stanley L. Jaki's phrase) of the public spirit have occurred over the centuries. The first necessity was an alchemy of mind itself. We have already suggested the reality of this thievery, however, as opposed to its appearance: subtle theft of community mind does not radically restructure the world; being continues being. What is radically

---

[1]Eric Voegelin, *Science, Politics and Gnosticism* (Chicago: Regnery, 1968); *From Enlightenment to Revolution* (Durham, NC: Duke University Press, 1975); *Order and History*, 5 vols. (Baton Rouge: Louisiana State University, 1956-1987), vol. 4.

affected is the state of being of the community mind and spirit, reductions which led us to name ours the Age of Acedia.

For the orthodox opponent of modern gnosticism, as we have said, Christ is descended into the flesh. His Passion is in the body. His Death and Resurrection are of the body. Thus in the Christian view Christ's victory is over death, not over the body, for the Christian believes that in Christ's death and resurrection, creation is established as good. So important is the belief that, as it encounters a stronger and stronger modern gnosticism that is militantly intent on dislocating mind from creation, the pressures on Christianity become such as to tempt the Christian to a severe literalness against these pressures. In his own extremism he is led to a rigidity of spirit and so easily loses sight of the fundamental stewardship of man in nature. What I have explicitly in mind is that conspicuous manifestation at this point of our war against modern gnosticism which has been labeled Protestant Fundamentalism, but we must speak here as well of fundamentalism wider in the Christian community than our usual association of it with the extreme splintering into sects. The immediate point is that, through such pressures toward literalism, one may incline to a gnosticism in the name of orthodoxy; the letter of the law becomes the reality. The confusion lies in this: though one shares particular being within the light of that Word which was in the beginning, one's own words do not consequently have the absolute authority of the Word, a truth easily blinked or forgotten in the pressure of the immediate battle, so that our letter of the law becomes not so much Christian witness as a counter gnosticism.

The heretical Gnostic, given his severe rationalism (to which heresy current Fundamentalism is most susceptible) cannot see the heresy, primarily because he believes his intellectual actions are the height of piety toward God. Believing such intellectual action the highest calling of his spirit, his whole being is thereby reduced to intellect, even though he call it "spirit." And within that intellect *gnosis* sits enthroned. This

Gnostic action, then, is a species of idol worship, though it has no concrete Baal. (When the secularist Robespierre raises a statue to Wisdom, he gives a concrete Baal for secular worship.) To the gnostic, the idol is the intellect's word, an ancient "Nominalist" error antecedent to those problems attendant upon its re-introduction into Western thought by Occam, and advanced by Descartes and others. In the name of God, the gnostic prevents himself from seeing his action as a presumptuous imitation of God's absolute power over being; nor may he see in what manner his own gnostic power is void of that mercy whereby creation is redeemed in Christ. One is dealing here with a "Fundamentalism" — a set of mind to which the multitudinous wonders and mysteries of creation itself are inaccessible. And it must be emphasized that the statement covers the secular gnostic no less than his ancient counterpart who addresses the world in the name of Christ. It is to the "fundamentalist" of an active secular intent that we now look, setting aside for the moment his Protestant Fundamentalist counterpart.

In my argument, I have depended in part on the history of the ancient Gnostic mind as explored by Hans Jonas in *The Gnostic Religion: The Message of the Alien God and the Beginnings of Christianity*.[2] Through his analysis, Jonas comes at last upon the kinship of that old heresy to the dominant secular philosophy that has commanded the modernist spirit. He uncovers parallels, somewhat to his surprise it seems to me, between his own most immediate intellectual history and that ancient version of it that seemed far removed at the outset of his study. In an epilogue to his Second Edition, called "Gnosticism, Existentialism, and Nihilism," he looks into Nietzsche, Heidegger, Sartre, and other carriers of that old intellectual malaise in the modern secular mind. Thus Jonas's book is a helpful analogue to any thorough exploration of gnosticism in the modern mind, a book made even

---

[2]Boston: Beacon Press, 1963.

more revealing if we read it in the light of Pieper's essay *On Hope.*

Concerning the gnostic's confusions, through pride of intellect, an elucidation of the virtue of hope may be as welcomed to the avowed secular mind as to the Christian Fundamentalist, assuming that both are seriously "on the way," that both are seriously concerned with the truth of being itself. Though we may not dwell on either Jonas or Pieper much further, from Pieper let us take a salient observation about our perversions of hope. He describes two states of hopelessness in the soul (which the secularist may wish to call "psyche" in its modern psychological meaning as opposed to its ancient gnostic sense). The first hopeless state we have already touched upon with the term *angst.* It is despair — that is, the soul's (or mind's) fearful anticipation of nonfulfillment, with an accompanying active descent into nothingness — into the very popular version of nothingness we call the Abyss in modern philosophy. That is the estate of soul in which we first encounter Haze Motes. He is caught up by intellectual presumption: by an act of will, the soul (mind) unwills to be what in reality it is, thus embarking upon the road to the perfection of non-existence. That is also Hulga's species of intellectual presumption as well, her embrace of nihilistic hopelessness which prompts her, with sardonic irony, to modify her surname Hopewell with Hulga as a replacement for Joy.

But it is the second state of hopelessness that reveals most about the dangers in the secular enthusiasms that are rampant in a variety of movements too numerous to name — Environmentalism, Communism, Socialism, Libertarianism, Feminism. It is this species of presumptuousness with which we must daily deal at the social and political levels of the body of community, so intrusive that the morning's junk mail solicits our membership in a different movement every day. Our Congress is besieged, though welcoming such "organized input" by gnostic organizations giving expert testimony on rarified aspects of the community body. Our problem in deciding allegiance among such legion bodies is discovering the ground held in common among them. Our disappointment is to discover that the common ground is a gnostic reading of man in the world, out of which is projected a dream-structure, a radical illusion of the body of the world. Hydra struggles with Proteus for dominance of the arena called existence.

This second species of presumptuousness violates the reality of personhood no less than does that which is religiously committed to nothingness, and may indeed have that first nihilistic presumption at its center. But its advantage over nihilism in capturing our consent lies in its seemingly being far removed from nihilism. It is a "positive" approach. It seems to offer hope by the strategy of focusing upon an appealing image of future fulfillment. Voegelin suggests the mechanism involved, pointing out that at least since Joachim of Flora in the twelfth century, stages toward the millennial have been seductive. The final and glorious age is always just ahead. The modern world, since the Renaissance, has been inundated with such stages — a historical past developed into an enlightened present through which a millennial future will be controlled. It is in Hegel, Marx, Darwin, etc., etc. With an authority justified by the intellect's persuasive reading of the past in relation to the present, the present is always an advance over the past (the Lucynell Crater position). The future is then projected in such a way as to command allegiance of those who have lost true intellectual vision — the gifts through which one develops his being under the intellect's ordinate command. We are caught in a millennial dream as if in a moral imperative.

In this second mode of hopelessness of spirit, personhood is violated in that the mode denies or obscures the constancy with which the particular person's being is itself "on the way" to fulfillment — is becoming. By substituting a dream end, a collective called "Humanity," the proper fulfillment of the person — the realization of the gifts of potentiality — are subverted.

Whatever the moment in history at which one falls into the gifts of personhood — past, present, future; our parents, ourselves, our children — the conditions of the gift command not to be violated lest the reality of both person and world be lost. Dreamland gnosis, then, violates personhood by submerging the discrete person (with his consent) in secular cause, however much the cause is deified by romantic or rationalistic dislocations from being. The promising person — promising in that he is on-the-way and has not secured his potential — is wooed to sacrifice the self to ideology. But that sacrifice requires dream images of one sort or another, through which one's sense of personhood may be dislocated. A future temporal point of fulfillment is colored by Eden imagery.

That is a necessary camouflage, whether propounded by Francis Bacon or Karl Marx; it is necessary precisely because the innate sense one has of personhood includes a hunger for fulfillment. Thus Karl Marx's famous dismissal of Christianity as an opiate of the people, deluding (in his view) the people by dreams of "Heaven." This innate hunger which requires "opiate" Marx recognizes as the key; he appropriates it to his own dream imagery of the Earthly Paradise, the "classless society." That appropriation is necessary if he is to persuade a sacrifice of the self to his ideology. For the inescapable reality of man's being is that one's sense of being "on-the-way" stimulates a legitimate hunger for fulfillment — legitimate in that it conforms to the gift of being in potential. It is this legitimate hunger that must be manipulated by secular gnosticism toward restructuring the world; without that manipulation, gnostic intent is powerless.

We need to remark again and underline the point that secular gnosticism distorts the discrete, particularizing gifts of being, those gifts whereby one is *this* person and no other. That is why it becomes important in gnostic thought to concentrate upon the idea of the heroic through an emphasis on spectacle. There is a considerable pantheon of gnostic saints whose sainthood is declared on the basis of sacrifice to an abstraction. As the abstraction is modified or replaced, under the necessities forced by reality, the saints and their legends are modified or obliterated. Concomitantly, the gnostic presumes, and must assert, that the transformation of being he pursues is inevitable. The sense of determinism in history is a corollary to the necessity of gnostic saints, since one of the realities of our being is that saints without a higher, omnipotent cause touching them are merely human animals. The mechanical (and thus lifeless) aspect of nineteenth century determinism receives some illusion of rescue from sheer mechanics when sacrificial persons (the gnostic saints) are elevated in the cause of mechanistic determinism. That combination, yielding saints of mechanism, Marx prepares us for with Hegelian tools. He "proves" a classless society to be an historical inevitability, and so appealing is the "classless society" that it becomes a cause suitable for the sacrifice of personhood. Thus one sacrifices oneself for an already inevitable, determined end, a most curious circumstance. But to presume the dream "society" inevitable, either at the level of the spirit as understood by the ancient Gnostic in his presumption of beatitude or at the naturalistic mechanistic level as understood by the gnostic Marxist, is a violation of reality. Most especially it is a violation of one's own being, whatever the consequences to the world larger than the self.

We must not forget, of course, the parallel violation of personhood in that "purer" gnosticism called Nihilism, the anticipation of a "perfection of non-being." In respect to the teleology of such a mind, neither should we forget that the particular person given to nihilism has not yet arrived at its consummation and so may turn and go another way, as Haze Motes does. The Nihilist or historical determinist is only on *a* way, not yet arrived at an end. In consequence of such a possible turning, out of either species of hopelessness, the prospect of sainthood may be contingently restored. And this is the most crucial point, which to miss dilutes that *caritas* proper to any mind's attempt to judge reality, especially the reality of personhood in discrete creatures. Even at a more subordinate level of judgment, at the level of "literary criticism," say, we may see that Miss O'Connor as artist is not so presumptuous as to intend by her made thing, her fiction, that we conclude her protagonist either lost or saved. He is only turned toward an openness among contingent possibilities. Treat the matter otherwise and the artist herself succumbs to a gnostic art, which in fact is widely practiced around Miss O'Connor and against which she distinguished her own attempts.

To see this point of contingency in her resolutions by contrast, recall the end of Sophocles' *Oedipus the King.* Sophocles has his chorus of little old men, representing the collective wisdom of man, declare as the final word:

> From hence the lesson learn ye,
> To reckon no man happy till ye witness
> The closing day; until he pass the border
> Which severs life from death, unscathed by sorrow.

The point in the contrast, the point Miss O'Connor intends in warning that Haze Motes in blinding himself is no Oedipus, is this: from the Christian position, we may count no man either lost or saved — totally condemned or totally rescued — so long as he is on-the-way, whatever the direction in which he is bound. This is a difference that establishes a gulf between the "Pagan" mind of the great poets and philosophers (Homer, the Tragedians, Plato, Aristotle, Virgil) and the Christian mind. The Christian is fearful of presumptuousness. If the Pagan mind looks at death darkly, as it tends to do, the Christian is inclined to joyful anticipation and so is tempted to conclude the rescue of his soul an inevitability. This is an abiding threat to the soul, from within itself, as opposed to the haunting fear of external fate that Sophocles's chorus voices. With fate the dominant anticipation, the only rescue seems to lie in the oblivion of death in Oedipus's world. What this comes down to at last is that in presumptuousness (that is, in false hope) — whether a presumption of fulfillment in non-being (nihilism) or of inevitable rescue out of one's being "on-the-way" — grace and its mysteries are denied. Even so, traditional words implying contingency are still with us, if but residually: "By the grace of God, I shall. . . ." We hold to the recognition, by the instinct for a fulfillment of personhood, knowing that in our finiteness we do not comprehend the mystery of our journey toward fulfillment. And we also no doubt hold that contingent word as talisman, wily primitives that we also are, as if against fate rather than in a recognition of the contingency of our journey toward an end. We shall arrive at our fullness, "The good Lord willing, *if the creek don't rise.*"

V

When we are persuaded of an inevitable rescue in fulfillment, the second mode of hopelessness, we are denying implicitly the finiteness of our personhood. The magical slight-of-hand which the secular gnostic must use in transferring this spiritual weakness to secular ends is to drown the person in gnostic idea. He must obliterate Dick and Jane in an enveloping "Cause" that is an end but which has no relation to beginnings. Thus the gnostic "Cause" is widely divorced from true Cause, namely from God. A vague "Humanity" usually serves the purpose, a temporary opiate in its effect. For the candidate in thrall to a secular gnosticism is likely to be caught up out of the personal issue on an emotional wave of enthusiasm. Dick and Jane are vaporized in the inclusiveness of "Humanity." It is a sacrifice to anonymity, in which respect it bears a parallel to the Nihilistic "perfection of non-being." It nevertheless maintains the illusion of the self's — the person's — having been dissolved into the borrowed godhead such as "Humanity," thus giving a religious tinge to secular ideologies. The impulse — if we may call it that — is our hunger for fulfillment in something other than our self, which the Christian understands to be paradoxical: in full surrender one is fulfilled. The legitimate desire is thus appropriated and distorted by the gnostic manipulator toward temporal ends. His gnostic neophyte is thus removed from the country of finitude, where the virtue of hope makes paradox acceptable, into the country of ironic contradiction of his dream by insistent reality. Except if he become simple mechanism, he is bound for nihilistic despair in the end.

In literature we observe this pattern of action in a protagonist such as Oedipus. The presumption of a conclusive fulfillment in a temporal cause (the rescue of Thebes by Oedipus's "gnostic" authority, his wisdom) we might well describe as a "tragic flaw." On the other hand, we are very hesitant to see that flaw in actual persons, those all about us who are caught up in social and political causes. If it is a presence in an Oedipus or a Lear, Sophocles and Shakespeare have but given us resonant imitations of actions in characters out of the realities of personhood; in those actions we ought to recognize ourselves more or less. That is, we do not deal merely with a "literary" element of character useful for the structuring of dramatic action in an aesthetically pleasing configuration, anymore than the dissociation of thought and feeling is merely a convenience if one wants to write a "romantic" poem or a "rational" poem. Aristotle well knew the point, through his exploration of the effect in tragedy he calls catharsis. For tragedy affects the audience beyond aesthetic effect. How "human" is Oedipus's confidence that, having solved the Sphinx's riddle, he is wise beyond ordinary men and therefore adequate to the rescue of Thebes. What we know, and what he discovers, is that he confuses cleverness with wisdom. In this respect, he might strike a more "kingly" presence on the "Wheel of Fortune" television show than in attempting to rescue Thebes from the plague.

We increasingly see enthusiastic presumption revealed, confidence that through cleverness we shall solve all manner of social and political problems; we shall solve those problems through a *gnosis* of our own discovery or devising. We shall rescue "Humanity" with the magic of formulae, whether the immediate problem be AIDS or poverty. It is no use our pretending this illusional gnosticism which is practiced on the social body is to be found only in Communist or Third World states; it is ours in democracies, in a spectrum from tacit assumption to overtly organized presumptions of inevitable fulfillment. And it has been increasingly so since we ceased to be

Christendom, or have ceased to believe our social and political callings in the world to be properly understood as under Christ's aegis.

We have remarked Hulga and Haze Motes as possessed by that pride of intellect which leads persons in hot pursuit of nothingness. They represent gnostic inclinations that are signally "modern," and so it is they who fascinate Miss O'Connor, given the fictional possibilities in such minds, as opposed to the possibilities in a mind like Mrs. Hopewell's. In a Mrs. Hopewell, one finds a rather simple version of the presumption of an accomplished fulfillment. Miss O'Connor pits a secular gnostic (Hulga) against a residual Christian Gnostic of the ancient sort (Mrs. Hopewell) in "Good Country People." But the spiritual complexities in her characters sometimes — often — involve both species of hopelessness within the same character, in which event the artful fiction is not only more complex in its action but more intellectually engaging. (We need reminding here of the distinction between spectacle and action. The action I speak of as complex is the movement of mind — the protagonist's — and not the external events we ordinarily and inexactly speak of as action.) That presumptuousness of an accomplished fulfillment is likely to be cast in its secular mode. That is, a Mrs. Turpin or a Mrs. May considers herself "saved" by having established legal title to the arena she has carved out of nature and separated from community. The complexity of existence, she then supposes, is effectively excluded, whether the proximate representation of that triumph over creation be a modern pig parlor or an established herd of cattle.

Each woman feels protected from unmannerly or dangerous intrusion. Mrs. May's confidence lies in her having exorcised spiritual being from her world. She has her property covered by an insurance policy and defended by Mr. Greenleaf's gun and so has nothing to fear (or rather, thinks she ought not to have anything to fear). She says she will die when she gets "good and ready." She has "worked" and not "wallowed," in contrast to the

Greenleafs, who "lived like the lilies of the field, off the fat that she [Mrs. May] struggled to put into the land." Mrs. May takes God's place in fattening nature as it were, depending on herself as the source of nature's bounty. She expects obeisance in return, at least from the Greenleafs, having given up on her own sons who disturbingly mirror her attitude toward existence. Ruby Turpin's legal grounds differ somewhat: she has a tacit contract with God, who is an absentee landlord not expected to meddle with her management. When in the denouement of "Revelation" that contract is not so much cancelled as declared nonexistent, not her farm but her soul lies devastated. Hers has been the position of the older brother to the prodigal son; all other people she sees as disgustingly prodigal, save the "nice" lady in the doctor's office. In her final humiliation, she goes to an encounter with God as wronged husbandman — wronged by God. She goes "single-handed, weaponless, into the battle."

To say that Mrs. Turpin has been humiliated in her encounter with the truth that she is "an old wart-hog" is to put the matter doubly. It means to her at first an embarrassment in public, through which she has lost respectability in a structured society that is comfortable to her. But her humiliation is at last at a theological, not at a popular, level, reminding us that, insofar as there has been any religious content to her language up to this final humiliation, it has managed only to echo old pieties from which spiritual virtues have been excluded. She has rested comfortably in her social position on the strength of the letter of piety, only to discover the letter is not enough, being empty of spirit. Her self-virtuous words have been scattered abroad to those in the doctor's office, out of her "good disposition," with no more charity than if husks were scattered before swine. When in response to her accusatory invocation of God she experiences the terrors of mercy, for the first time she discovers herself in nowise forearmed against mercy's assault. The stunning vision is that all souls like hers and Claude's, those "who . . . had always had a little of everything and the God-given wit to use it right" appear last on the road to rescue. They are preceded by "whole companies of white-trash, clean for the first time in their lives, and bands of black niggers in white robes, and battalions of freaks and lunatics shouting and clapping and leaping like frogs."

Mrs. Turpin in her humiliation finds that she is rear guard to a raggle-taggled but triumphant army of the Lord. With Mrs. Turpin we glimpse the Church Militant becoming the Church Triumphant. As Mrs. May's gnostic insurance, an inadequate piece of the crumbling secular rock on which she has built, is violently cancelled, so Mrs. Turpin's Puritan contract with God has been nullified. Mrs. Turpin is returned to the world which now breathes as she has never sensed it breathing, with a presence awful — that is with a presence that humiliates the soul to the level where recovery becomes possible through awe. She hears in "the invisible cricket chorus" about her as she makes her way back to Claude and their supper, voices like those of "souls climbing up . . . and shouting hallelujah." The conclusion leaves Mrs. Turpin in a literally darkening world, but one which is for the first time beginning to throb with the light of its being. Nature, hers and Claude's farm, can never be again quite what it has been for Mrs. Turpin, though whether or not she grows spiritually from this point may be set aside from our judgment as inappropriate to fiction's limits.

The story does, however, encourage our contrasting it to another fictional revelation given a character, a revelation also made in and through nature. It is a story Miss O'Connor knew very well, Hawthorne's "Young Goodman Brown." Hawthorne's young man comes to a devastating encounter with evil in nature, after which he continues all life long to be haunted by a faint but lingering satanic laughter out of the body of the world. He lives longer than Mrs. May, probably longer than will Mrs. Turpin. But he has so shut himself off from the complexity of existence that he can hear no cricket hallelujah choruses, nor encounter that destroying love out of nature that Mrs. May glimpses for an instant. When Brown is "borne to his grave a hoary corpse, followed by Faith, an aged woman, and children and grandchildren, a goodly procession, besides neighbors not a few, they carved no hopeful verse upon his tombstone, for his dying hour was doom." We are to suppose, that is, that he dies in nihilistic hopelessness, as he has lived in it after his dark night in the forest.

An alarming public development has occurred since the death of Flannery O'Connor in 1964, in respect to presumptuous hope of fulfillment, the presumption that turns hope to hopelessness. Here is alchemy indeed, because hope turned hopelessness usurps the limits of hope as circumscribed by reality: the reality of man's being on-the-way. There is, in this public development of the past two decades, the new — or at least more obvious — appearance of organized presumption. Whether there will be happy issue out of such organized and institutionalized intellectual error seems in the balance. Its spectacle is everywhere about us, cast in seeming conflict with the Mrs. Mays or Lucynell Craters of the world, who for their part advance a multitude of social and political and economic causes with secular gnostic fervor. It is this increasingly active opposition to secularism, made in the name of God, that we next address — an opposition being mounted in what has been recently described as the "naked public square." The phrase is Richard John Neuhaus's, developed in his widely discussed book *The Naked Public Square: Religion and Democracy in America,*[1] in which he examines the confrontation between what we have here called modern gnosticism and an ancient Gnosticism in modern dress. (These are not his terms.) The presumptuousness we encounter in a militantly religious opposition to that pervasive secularism which is busily eroding executive, legislative, and judicial institutions. It declares itself Christianity but reveals itself at heart to be but a modern version of that ancient Gnostic heresy. From an orthodox point of view, then, we seem to be

---

[1]Grand Rapids, MI: Wm. B. Eerdmans, 1984.

observing two gnostic armies clashing in an intellectual night, each professing to be the true light-bearer. It is to ancient Gnosticism in modern garb that we now turn to juxtapose it to the secular gnosticism we have been discussing, the better to see each.

vi

In this decade (the 1980s) it has become a popular tack to single out the Fundamentalist Christian for the role of buffoon or Neanderthal, picturing him as given to a blind reactionary assault upon an enlightened society. I shall rather speak of him as a continuing manifestation of the ancient Gnostic, and as such sharing intellectual error with his avowed enemy, the secular gnostic. I would wish it understood that, in degrees varying from the subtle to the blatant, one finds the same ancient Gnostic ground in religious positions widely removed from Fundamentalist sects, especially in those formal, "mainline" churches in which the "moderate's" is the louder voice. In that portion of Christendom, the moderate position often proves less given to a Christian position than to the secular gnosticism which has gradually come to co-opt the idea of moderation. For "moderation" is sometimes a clever strategy, nevermore than when intellect is in decay. In a decaying climate of mind, the appeal to "reason" is more often than not an appeal to "feeling" miscalled reason.

Miss O'Connor, we heard her say, finds Nihilism in and out of the Church, though that within is hardly likely to recognize itself as nihilistic. The presence of gnostic problem-solvers in the "main-line" Protestant churches is now somewhat notorious, especially as that element comes to focus in the World Council of Churches, to speak nothing of its presence in pastoral pronouncements on political and economic issues by various colleges of Bishops. The drift of gnostic pollution even affects the more limited philosophical and theological arena of the churches as might be apparent to examination. (I have suggested that St. Thomas's *Summa* can be, has been, and is used in gnostic ways that would shock him.) The division from orthodoxy exists then in the Roman as well as in the Protestant church. But it is of the Protestant Fundamentalist that I wish to speak, taking him as a conspicuous figure in the gnostic manipulations of orthodoxy whose counterpart one might find as well in Rome, Canterbury, or Flannery O'Connor's middle Georgia independents.

I have two reasons for this limited approach. First, it is in the interest of whatever light may be shed on Flannery O'Connor's uses of Southern Fundamentalism in her fiction. She often casts the Southern Fundamentalist as mediate antagonist, as the agent of grace to her protagonists — such characters as Old Tarwater in *The Violent Bear It Away* or Asa Hawks in *Wise Blood*, Asa being a more intense and complex presence in that novel than usually supposed. In her letters and in her essays she speaks repeatedly of her interest in the Southern Fundamentalist, her incisive but often sympathetic view a cause of bafflement to some, given her strict Thomism. Often her readers, especially those looking at her from a position understood to be more or less orthodox, are much puzzled. In response to that misunderstanding, she wrote many letters and perhaps most of her talks and essays. Those pieces are addressed to an elect audience separate from the audience intended for her fiction. If the audience to which her fiction is directed is that one which concludes God is dead, her letters and talks are aimed at an audience still professing a belief. But this audience is puzzled by the depths of her interest in the "fundamentalist" protagonist. It is the depth, the action in her characters, and not their outward appearances that is important, for many writers, especially of "Southern" fiction, have peopled their fictions with Fundamentalists. The difference is that ordinarily a Fundamentalist character (see Erskine Caldwell, for instance) provides spectacle, event, and not actions of mind at the level of Miss O'Connor's interest. She is concerned with dramatic action at a spiritual and intellectual level, not with spectacle and surface

event. She speaks of this interest very clearly in a letter to
William Sessions: "One of the good things about Protestantism
[and she has in mind the Southern variety of Protestant
Fundamentalism] is that it always contains the seeds of its own
reversal."[1]

Put in other terms, the Protestant character is the more
richly dramatic as he contends with grace. He is open to two
lines of movement in his being "on the way," "at one end to
Catholicism, and at the other to unbelief," as she says. But as we
discover him in *medias res* in the fiction, he is anxiously
concerned for his relation to God, concerned with whether to
reject God in unbelief or accept God toward a fullness such as
that understood by orthodoxy. The Southerner in general shares
with the Thomist this sense of being in the middle of the journey.
He is concerned with the journey's end. This is the point Miss
O'Connor makes in speaking of the South as certainly "Christ-
haunted" even though it is not "Christ-centered." (She would
have been very much aware, of course, that she writes the words
we have just quoted to a recent convert from Southern
Protestantism to Catholicism.)

At the level of spiritual reality — that is, at the level of the
actual manifestations of Christ-haunted persons she knows in the
South and particularly in central Georgia — she sees in these
troubled souls an insistence upon fundamental questions that
must be asked and answered in one way or another. Given her
own orthodox "Fundamentalism," she is the better attuned to
what is all about her in her South and concludes the South to
have a different spiritual climate from the one she knew in Iowa
or Connecticut or New York. Her Misfit puts the question to a
lukewarm Protestant mind, the Grandmother in "A Good Man Is
Hard to Find": either Christ was what he said he was and did
what he is said to have done, or he was a liar and con-artist. This

---

[1]"To William Sessions," 29 September 1960, *The Habit of Being*, p.
41.

is an extreme putting of the question, but it is put as much by Miss O'Connor from her own "Fundamentalist" position as by the Misfit. (Compare her remark on the Eucharist: if it is only a sign "I say to hell with it.") She forces the question upon Rayber in *The Violent Bear It Away*. Rayber is an instance of the secular gnostic we have described. The question is most tellingly put in her novel by that Fundamentalist preacher, Old Tarwater, whom she speaks of as a "natural Catholic," a presence acceptable to her beyond his fictional advantages.

The second reason I choose to focus on the Fundamentalist as representative of the old Gnostic heresy is that I myself have a native sympathy for that movement and would wish to see it address its gnostic tenor and deal with the weakness inherent in it. In addition, it is at this moment the most effective rallying point against the dominant secular gnosticism of our world. While I share Miss O'Connor's sympathetic interest, I do not, anymore than does she, subscribe to the errors increasingly divisive in it and so increasingly destructive of its potential effectiveness. For brevity's sake let me engage the "born again" mentality in that movement as the most obvious evidence of a presumptuousness that must prove spiritually fatal to the Fundamentalist soul caught up by enthusiasm into an idea. It *is* an idea raised by intellect. The "born-again" idea has as its implicit meaning as advanced by aggressive Fundamentalism a presumption of hope already fulfilled; in consequence it is one of the species of hopelessness we discussed above. The Misfit's demand for an immediate decisive conclusion of the matter is typical of the general problem, given the inescapable reality of the individual soul's being "on the way." Either Christ was what he said he was or he wasn't, and I ought to be shown by some outer action or sign or some persuasive emotional state which one it is.

In this life man is properly described in the concept *status viatoris*, not *status comprehensoris*; so long as he is in life he is in a state of being on-the-way, not in a state of beatitude. The Misfit is to be understood in these terms, which is why Miss O'Connor can suggest it possible that the old lady's final gesture to him could very well "turn him into the prophet he was meant to become." Haze, too, wants some irrefutable assurance that the secular, animalistic absolute is justified; he wants his faith — that there is no such thing as sin — to be certified by authority. Because of his uncertainty, we realize that he is not wholly given to the nihilism he professes. Haze's integrity, Miss O'Connor suggests in her note to the second edition of *Wise Blood*, lies in his inability to get rid of "the ragged figure that moves from tree to tree in the back of his mind," the figure of Christ. He is not then a figure of man as a determined creature in either a Calvinistic or a mechanistic manner. On the point, Miss O'Connor reminds us that "free will does not mean one will, but many wills conflicting in one man." There is no reason out of man's experience of his wills in conflict, then, that may justify a conclusion that being "born again" certifies rescue out of those wills in conflict within the self and against the world. Haze reflects precisely this heresy in the "born-again" idea until rebuked by the reality of his own nature, though he expresses it in an unusual way. Or rather, he expresses it in a way now rather more usual among us. He is a "born-again" nihilist. He anchors his faith in mechanistic nature, rejecting spirit, only to discover a deeper will in him for an anchor of spirit as well. His *way*, his gnostic formula, is the secular one, but in spite of his attempts to embrace that idea fully, he cannot. He admits at last that he is not clean, his earlier insistence to the contrary being the born-again secular gnostic error in him.

Haze, discontent with his own "Church Without Christ," finds that his "born again" faith in material existence has no stamp of authority stronger than his own assertion, his "way of saying something." Miss O'Connor remarks to Shirley Abbott that "It is popular to believe that in order to see clearly one must

believe nothing."[2] It is an address to existence which "may work
well enough if you are observing cells under a microscope," but
this born-again scientific vision, absorbed by Haze through
intellectual osmosis from the climate of the age, works not at all
either in fictional reality nor in our own experiences of life.
(Increasingly we discover it an impossible position, even when
one is attempting to observe cells under a microscope.)

The Fundamentalist position hardly appears to be one
established by "gnosis," when viewed from the position of the
"moderate." "Knowledge" in this view hardly seems a term
appropriate to describe a religious position which appears so
little given to the intellectual grounds of its own position and so
fiercely derisive of all intellectualism. But the secret knowledge
it holds to against the generality of intellectual opposition —
against an intellectualism which alternately laments and
anathematizes Fundamentalism — is taken into the
Fundamentalist's heart through the intellect. It is embraced by a
knowing act, whose spectacle is the emotional assertion of
knowing a secret. One is dealing with intellectual act in the
Fundamentalist, however undisciplined that professing mind may
appear in defending its secret knowledge. In addition, the
Fundamentalist makes public argument in its defense no less
than in its attack upon the secularist. There is intellectual
engagement, however flawed the argument in respect to the
formal principles of argument. In addition to which, we observe,
the Fundamentalist holds his position to be the one *reasonable*
one.

The flaw in the "born-again" idea in my viewpoint, which I
believe to be the orthodox position, lies in the "born-again"
Christian's inordinate trust in God's mercy, whereby it is assumed
that the soul is, by being "reborn," actually and absolutely rescued
from the reality of its being in the world, the reality of its being
"on the way" with the continuing necessity of being momently

---

[2]"To Shirley Abbot," 17 March 1956, *The Habit of Being*, p. 147.

born again. So long as one is in the world, there is the contingent possibility of failure, of a falling away, with every breath. That is why the "back-slider" is such a nagging problem for the extremist in the Fundamentalist movement. Fundamentalism feels compelled to declare its church a collection of the saved, rather than a gathering of sinners to be saved through continuing grace, sustained through that grace in a hope beyond the hopelessness of presumption. Those moderates, annually in conflict with the extremists at conventions (to the general delight of the media), are perhaps less exercised by the spiritual issue than by a social embarrassment. One suspects this is so because the moderate tends to be a secularist at heart, as the Fundamentalist charges him with being. So far as I have noticed (though I have not noticed all), the issue is seldom engaged in the public conventions on theological grounds. The war is waged rather at the level of political governance, theological issues put offstage, as if obscene in an ancient sense.

Even granting the avowedly secular position of our pluralistic society, as opposed to the Fundamentalist religious one, we must heed the necessity of being momently born-again, at least at the intellectual level. The born-again idea is one the secular gnostic may take only as figurative. But increasingly, he must go at least this far, since there is overwhelming evidence of his flawed intellectual readings of reality. For his own intellectual address to reality is no less a born-again presumptuousness than is the Fundamentalist's. From the Soviet Five Year Plans to our War on Poverty, the failure of intellect to restructure existence is inescapable. He, too, must be constantly dealing with a back-sliding. The presumption of the secular (as opposed to the transcendental Gnostic) is refuted by the complexity of reality in alarming ways. For neither Fundamentalist nor the secularist has a purchase upon grace from his intellectual authority. The spiritual, transcendental Gnostic in effect declares an irreversible contract made with God, whereby God is reduced to a contracting party out of his omnipotence. (The Fundamentalist may go only so far as asserting that he "feels" such a contract.) On the other hand, the secular gnostic takes grace as an uncaused power in intellect itself. Possessing it by will, he intends to manipulate the world of being into an image of that manipulating intellect. The two are not blood brothers, for that would anchor them in reality, but mind brothers. They have descended to us through historical successions one might describe as a laying on of idea rather than the laying on of hands. The origins are ancient, but let us look at a relatively recent source in our national history, a very limited version of this general descent of idea in the West. I have in mind our New England Puritan heritage as a source of both secular and theistic gnosticism.

vii

In interesting and decisive ways, the Puritan contract between William Bradford and God, made on a ship off New England shores, brings together both strands of gnosticism. That contract casts long shadows in our national life. With the gradual separation of a theistic emphasis upon a City on the Hill from the mere city, through the actions and arguments of minds from Winthrop to Jonathan Edward to Benjamin Franklin to Ralph Waldo Emerson, the two "forces" in that early Gnostic contract find themselves aligned against each other — secular pragmatism opposed to religious Fundamentalism. Defective gnostic seed, I am suggesting, was planted in the national mind very early, and its variety in germination and growth has fed American literature, politics, and social actions ever since. We witness at the national level the awkward encounter between the divergent gnosticisms and the stumbling attempts to reconcile them through executive, legislative, judicial struggles in the 1980s. (The history of this separation, as reflected in particular minds, is a major theme in my *Why Hawthorne Was Melancholy*,[1] in consequence of which I here make only summary statement, citing that work for support.)

Through gnostic presumptions, then — whether as ancient as Origen's or as recent as John Winthrop's — thought becomes the absolute in the gnostic mind. This is the "incarnational" act whereby body is rejected so that body (i.e., the created world, including the gnostic's own body) may be reconstituted. The world's body is reduced to *fact* or *idea*, whether in the interest of making it an inert stairway to the transcendent for the Puritan

---

[1](La Salle, IL: Sherwood Sugden, 1984).

mind or a closed machine, the tinker toy of the secular gnostic. In either direction, the gnostic declares power over being, the one in the name of God, the other in the name of his own power over nature through fact and idea. What both actions overlook, a failure whose consequences bear heavily upon us at this point in our history, is that such an address to creation calls in question both the existence of the created world and the goodness of the Creator of that world. This is so in spite of the ancient reminder that God Himself finds his creation good and in spite of the long searching by our theological mind from the Church Fathers through Augustine and Thomas which insists that, indeed, creation is good. Though poised in public war against each other, the two gnostic camps in concert wound a sacredness in creation.

Implicit in the gnostic position, in consequence of this oversight, is a Manicheanism as a necessity to gnostic thought, at least insofar as the gnostic mind is unable to maintain an absolute solipsism. (A mind cannot logically or practically maintain a solipsistic position so long as it consents to its body's breathing, eating, sleeping — a point Socrates realized a long time ago.) Yet the evil or recalcitrant world, for Puritan gnostic or secular gnostic, must have its being accounted for in some way, the mind itself nagging and nagging until the problem is addressed. On the one hand our Puritan gnostic has great difficulty establishing any ordinate love of creation proper in relation to the health of mind and soul; his constant fear is that *any* delight — especially in wine, food, song, sex — for the things "of" the world is necessarily excessive. The dilemma is a constant in folk humor, for instance the stories about the preacher at Sunday dinner eating his hosts poor; into the poor house. It is a constant in the evening papers as well as in the disturbed stories of some minister's sexual violation of some of his flock.

On the other hand, the secular gnostic, whose god is his own intellect, has no stay at all against an inordinate love of material existence. Sometimes he develops a sophisticated detachment from the world of things, an assumption (and consumption) of things at their most rarified. The refinements of hedonism contrast sharply to the occasional grossness of indulgence in the worldly by the Puritan gnostic, though the root cause in each is the same. Thus the indulgence in the worldly reflected in the advertisements of worldly goods in *The New Yorker* or *Gourmet: The Magazine of Good Living* seems further removed from the jokes about the Preacher's Sunday gluttony than is actual, for the problem in both is the loss of an ordinate love of being. On an ascending scale, one moves from tea to wine to Scotch to — Perrier?   The pure essence pursued is pursued through Nominalism, that convenience to modern gnosticism whereby mind sets itself apart from existence on the authority of its power through words. Existence may be allowed some controlled return to a "presence" (to use a current secular philosophy's term) as in a refined hedonism, or it may be savaged as by gluttony. But in either address, existence is invaded through the power of words, whether from the Bible understood literally or from nihilistic philosophy. For there is a species of "Puritanism" controlled or uncontrolled in secular gnosticism, which shares a fear with the theistic Puritanism, a fear of existence.

In either gnostic abuse of creation, creation itself is left unaccounted for in its fullness, the gnawing and almost subliminal recognition of which is an uneasiness with creation. The Fundamentalist is not quite content to declare existence absolutely evil, but has no rational ground to conclude otherwise. Still, he is caught in the necessities of eating and drinking, and given to other of the body's pulls to creation. He sympathizes mightily with Saint Paul's lament of the thorn in the flesh. But, says the conciliatory secular gnostic, suppose that evil could be declared an illusion? Sin would then be abolished. (*Pace* Haze Motes.) Perhaps then a way is at last clear to make of the world what it ought to have been, had it been made by the intellect of man rather than being merely uncaused cause, that accidental existence. That is the direction Ralph Waldo Emerson takes in adjusting his own Puritanism and laying the ground for the establishment of the American intelligentsia. It was through Puritan gnosticism secularized that grace was finally separated from nature, an operation whereby nature is consequently understood to have whatever life it has from man's intellect. Intellect is the new agent of grace in a secular world. Dead nature becomes prime matter for gnostic restructuring of the world by *fact* in service to *idea*, the two becoming the adjustable pliers that twist existence into a machine suitable to the will.

Miss O'Connor herself sees Emerson as a crucial figure in the dislocation, though she does not dwell on him. She remarks only that "When Emerson decided, in 1832, that he could no longer celebrate the Lord's Supper unless the bread and wine were removed, an important step in the vaporization of religion in America was taken, and the spirit of that step has continued apace." She might well have added that, in his "American Scholar," Emerson lays out a program whereby not only religion but nature itself is vaporized. It is a document dear to the heart of the intelligentsia of the American academy — some understanding full well what Emerson is actually saying, some only approving because it is the enlightened thing to do, like serving crepes or Perrier.

Emerson's rejection of bread and wine at his version of the Lord's Supper is a very conspicuous instance of his Puritan rejection of nature. For him nature is a thing to be used by the will in the interest of an absoluteness of the self. His "American Scholar," plus his address to the Harvard Divinity School, provides scriptural authority for secular gnosticism, which trickles down into the popular spirit from the academy, though the popular spirit feeds on Emerson from *Bartlett's Familiar Quotations* rather than from the "scripture" itself. (He is, and has been from the beginning, a favorite as filler for newspaper makeup editors.) If Thoreau to some extent and Hawthorne and Melville rather extensively oppose Emersonian thought, he yet affects our letters more than they. A version of Puritan thought *via* Emerson is present in an agitated way in the most popular of our poets, Robert Frost. Frost modifies the Puritan version of the wilderness as satanic antagonist. He follows Emerson, but with severe reservations and disclaimers. Emerson's Puritan position takes nature as matter (actually, less than matter) to be used to serve the glory of man, rather than the glory of God as was Winthrop's position. For Frost, nature is antagonist, less virulent than in the Puritan version, a more active presence than in Emerson's version. Frost dramatizes a dualism through a game which mind plays against nature, asserting that nature's action is a pull to formlessness, against which pull mind asserts form. The game is constant, with no end to it. Man's mind largely sets the rules, though this means ultimately that mind sets up a game it plays with itself, like a chess game with the imaginary partner nature. In Frost, there is little sense of man's being on the way, *homo viator*. The best one can hope for is a draw in the game at a point we call death.[2]

One discovers a secular gnosticism in our national popular mind, reflected in much of its literature, that has developed in that mind out of the fragmentation of Puritan gnosticism; it is the new religion endemic. Its priest is intellect, whose robes, though now much tattered, are those of science. Its mysteries are facts derived from machines and used through the machinery of mind to reconstruct being. By machine I mean those literal extensions of mind into gears and pulleys and computers; but I also mean most particularly the machine of mind itself, manipulated as machine in the restructuring of consciousness — of consciousness taken both individually and collectively. I trust it understood that my objection is not to machines themselves, but to the presumption that nature and mind alike are machines to be manipulated, the manipulator usually finding some way to exclude himself from the mechanistic vision of existence.[3]

---

[2] See the poem he wished set at the end of his life's work, "In Winter in the Woods Alone."

[3] C.S. Lewis remarks that Freudianism can explain everything but Freud, a point that did not escape Jung. On the point, see George B.

One finds the modern gnostic at his most dangerous to community health, not as he deals with the body of the world through literal machines in a consumer society, but as he deals with that machinery of "social consciousness." For the gnostic, it is the collective consciousness that must be reconstructed by adjustments in the mind's machinery if this new religion is to prevail, a religion built on a faith that all existence including mind is mechanistic. That control established, it is presumed, all else will follow, including the control of body at the level of consumerism. We ought to remember here that there is a fundamental level of gnostic competition between "capitalism" and "communism" in which both are "consumer-oriented" in like gnostic ways. In neither is accounting made of the spiritual dimension of existence, as found in persons, in the things of nature, or in the things made of nature by persons. When the virtues of capitalism are argued at the secular level, capitalism itself is most suspect, a point recognized by Michael Novak, who attempts to counter it in *The Spirit of Democratic Capitalism.*

One must contend not only with gnostic entrepreneurs of made things in a consumer world (the Soviet and Third World countries no less that Western democracies); one most disturbingly must deal with the gnostic entrepreneur of words who is bent on a fundamental deconstruction and reconstruction of mind, the blueprint for which reconstruction is an idea regnant in a single or collective gnostic mind, a mystery possessed and to be executed upon creation. One has, then, two species of Fundamentalism in contention over the body of the world, gnostic twins born of a misreading of the nature of existence itself. That is why I suggest that we witness, at every level of our social life, the battle of ignorant armies, each contending its justification to be the true light of intellect. Each competes to subscribe the residual gnostic presence in the public mind, the

---

Hogenson's *Jung's Struggle with Freud* (Notre Dame: University of Notre Dame Press, 1983).

one under such banners as "Moral Majority," the other under no such common shibboleth but often characterized as "Liberal" or "Moderate"; his is the "respectable" intellectual position that shys from label.

viii

A refutation of modern gnosticism depends upon the reassertion of the complexity of existence, especially in regard to man himself, against the systematic reduction of man to animalistic nature or determined machine. The reduction is pervasive, as in this introductory dogma to sociology as science that falls to hand, Peter L. Berger's *Invitation to Sociology*: "Society not only determines what we do but also what we are."[1] This is the understanding of sociology at the level of a Mrs. Lucynell Crater, the unfortunate truth being that it is the level officially taught to undergraduates *en masse* from prestigious podiums. We may assert with growing confidence, however, that the current secular gnostic dogma which is pronounced by Berger, though raised to the level of dogma as the "respectable" intellectual position by nineteenth century science, is now brought into serious question, and most effectively so from within science itself, particularly by the so-called "hard" sciences. There is increasingly within the scientific community a recognition of a need for metaphysical resolution to questions that defy the rational intellect. Particle physics is most conspicuous in this concern, though the concern grows even in the soft-sciences that rose to authority on the coattails of physics and chemistry and biology. In ten years — may we dare hope? — that new metaphysical attention will have reached the teaching level in colleges and universities.

Meanwhile, one keeps calling attention to the unrest in science. David Berlinski, in his recent *Black Mischief: The*

---

[1]*Invitation to Sociology: A Humanistic Perspective* (Garden City, NY: Doubleday Anchor, 1963), p. 93.

Mechanics of Modern Science[2], observes that "science has historically been most successful when it ignores the grossness of complexity and treats instead of a sparse and elegant universe in which point masses, for example, replace planets, and numbers come to stand for properties." He examines with scientific skepticism — an old virtue in science much in decline since its triumph over the public mind — the sparse and therefore elegant paradigms of molecular biology, psychology, and the several sciences that concentrate on the nature of man. He finds reductionism yielding a dogma no less pervasive of scientific thought in these specializations than in astronomy. The excision of a sparse and elegant paradigm of being from the complexity of being, and the declaration of that refined model as dogma is, of course, untenable, given the principle of objectivity at the heart of science. A religious conviction of certitude in matters scientific is the devil's temptation to the scientist at his trade: a *rest* in conclusion is the death of science, no less than of the soul on its way through the world. That is why science can contribute to satisfying but cannot fully satisfy the soul's hunger for rest in certitude. Science may bring one only to the point where at least metaphysics becomes a necessity.

If this be so, one concludes that the dogmatic scientist Berlinski reveals is himself a fundamentalist, his position establishing a hopelessness of presumption, a pretense to finality, not unlike the position we have described in the "born-again" religious Fundamentalist. It becomes a point of some irony, then, when these two Fundamentalists collide. Berlinski demonstrates how the explicit term *dogma* is embraced by neo-Darwinian pursuits of evolution into the mysteries of DNA, the term *dogma* literally attached to theoretical ideas to assert them an established conclusion, when they are only beliefs that are not actually scientifically demonstrated principles. Darwinian theory is and will be (short of blinding divine revelation) circular in its

---

[2](New York: William Morrow and Company, Inc., 1986).

premise, one statement of which circularity Berlinski makes: "Those characteristics that are relatively fit are relatively fit in virtue of the fact that they have survived." This is to say that "those traits that survived survived," not much of an advance upon an article of faith, leaving Darwinian evolution "fact-heavy, law-poor" and "surprisingly resistant to confirmation." To address the question through the mysteries of micro-biology is only to encounter the basic impasse in more complicated form. As Berlinski puts it, "To talk blithely of evolution in strings is to assume the completion of the first two steps in biological evolution: the emergence of lifelike systems from inorganic matter, and the adventitious creation of modern biological systems of replication and genetic information."

With these fundamental neo-Darwinian problems in mind, Berlinski observes the so-called Little Rock "Scopes Two" Trial (1982), which pitted evolutionist against Fundamentalist. He observes of the neo-Darwinian position: "If mathematical physics offers a vision of reality at its most comprehensive [and yet incomplete], the Darwinian theory of evolution, like psychoanalysis, Marxism, or the Catholic faith, comprises instead a system of belief. Like hell itself . . . each such system looks essentially sturdy from the inside. Standing at dead center, most people have considerable difficulty in imagining that an outside exists at all." Berlinski is, obviously, concerned that his detached and uncommitted position not be overlooked; hence the playful analogy of these systems of belief, including "the Catholic faith," to hell itself. But, though little sympathetic to religious belief on theistic ground, he is more unsympathetic to religious belief with no ground at all. He reports the opinion of a star witness, summoned by the Fundamentalist side in the trial: "An astrophysicist by training, and hence superior in status to any of the biologists [at the trial], [Chandra] Wickramasinghe compared the Darwinian theory in point of plausibility to the thesis that a Boeing 747 might arise spontaneously from a junkyard struck by a tornado. . . . The account of creation by Genesis I:1

Wickramasinghe dismissed with a snort. 'Obvious twaddle,' I thought I heard him say at the airport, before his supporters reminded him just who had paid for his roundtrip ticket."

Given the hierarchy of prestige within the scientific establishment suggested by Berlinski,[3] an astrophysicist is to biologists as the Archbishop of Canterbury to the parish priest, and it is the Darwinian parish priests we last hear from in his account. "In the end the Darwinians agreed that the Darwinian theory was quite beyond controversy among reasonable men; but why then were they there, explaining once more to an audience of bewildered and resisting laymen how it is that time and chance work their will in an ancient world?" More and more we begin to realize that the originating minds of this new faith, the continuing body of Darwinian scientists, appear in considerable disarray over the fundamental meaning of existence; they cling to a mystery increasingly eroded by their own discoveries, namely the accidental emergence of life whose ontological questions are begged.[4] In this light, the confident assertion of Mrs. Lucynell Crater, in Flannery O'Connor's "The Life You Save May Be Your Own," becomes less and less tenable in that intellectual community that thinks itself far removed from her piney-woods scrub farm: the monks of old, she says with authority, "wasn't as advanced as we are."

We have used Mrs. Crater, a fictional character, to represent the trickle-down effect in society of dogmatic scientific ideology, an ideology whose source is the gnostic intellectual community. This is to say that the effect erodes the fabric of society at every level, reaching even into the backwaters of society. That makes possible Miss O'Connor's own species of black mischief, the holding up of a Mrs. Crater as mirror to the reigning gnostic mind in a shocking confrontation. Perhaps, then,

---

[3]See pages 86-87.
[4]See not only Berlinski, but Owen Barfield's treatment of the position in *Saving the Appearances: A Study in Idolatry* (New York: Harcourt, Brace, Jovanovich, nd).

we may engage the monkish rubric that man is created in the image of God and attempt its rehabilitation. We shall certainly find it less necessary now than it would have been fifty years ago to make apology to the Lucynell Craters of the world. But we must first, however, look to the world's dislocation and appropriation by the Lucynells.

The Christian rubric — man as created in God's image — when given a slight but decisive variation by nineteenth century gnostic thought, became generally triumphant, though it is now radically in question to the confusion of the public mind. If that gnostic shift of the rubric has not always been advanced openly (how could it be, since its concern was a subversion of the popular mind to the new religion), the variation and its consequences are inescapable. The process of its thought over three centuries may be put something like this: If God existed (as Puritan Gnosticism holds), one grants that man must necessarily exist in some respect in the image of God. But, as the new science shows, God does not exist, man being himself biological accident. Therefore "God" exists only in the image of man's intellectual perfection, projected upon the world by intellect itself; intellect must now take charge of and order accidental existence, including its own existence. The argument (*vide* Emerson's as exemplum) is made comfortable by our being assured that such an image is worthy of worship. Marxism, for instance, is undeniably committed to this assurance. Therefore man is the most suitable God. The manipulation of being by intellect these past three hundred years is summed up in this redaction. But a critical examination of the argument — scientific or philosophical or theological — shows it untenable except through a very rudimentary fundamentalist faith in the assertion itself. One interested in the meticulous examination of its inadequacies at the philosophical level — the point at which one should begin with a "scientific" address in the oldest sense of that term — will find that examination made in such works as Voegelin's *From Enlightenment to Revolution*, Barfield's *Saving the*

Appearances: A Study in Idolatry, Niemeyer's *Between Nothingness and Paradise*, Jaki's *The Road of Science and the Ways of God*, Gilson's *From Aristotle to Darwin and Back Again*, Michael Denton's *Evolution: A Theory in Crisis*, and a considerable number of searching studies that promise to make ours the Second Scholastic Age when reviewed by our successors.

In the light of these and other examinations, let us take as a suitable point of departure in opposing gnostic heresy a long-neglected monkish understanding of the nature of mind itself. We shall see that it is Miss O'Connor's understanding as well. The gnostic simplifications of the little world of man, in the interest of sparse and elegant "universes," provides the intellectual milieux of her fiction, to which she gives local habitation and name. Thus her Bible salesman is a "born" Nihilist-Existentialist, in contrast to Hulga, who is only a "born-again" Nihilist-Existentialist, having needed formal doctoral work to reach the position. Haze Motes is a backwoods Nietzsche. With deliberate step, then, we take up the medieval understanding of the mystery of mind to discover the inadequacies of gnostic presumptions residual in Hulga and Haze and other O'Connor characters.

The scholastic distinguished two modes in the action of man's thought, the *ratio* and the *intellectus*. That distinction is fundamental to Miss O'Connor, though she does not use those technical terms. She would nevertheless have known them from her reading of Josef Pieper's *Leisure: The Basis of Culture*, and she uses their meanings quite inescapably. When she does so, her terms are more general; she uses those still in popular use with a vestigial presence of the old distinctions. She advises Cecil Dawkins, for instance, "Don't mix up thought-knowledge with felt-knowledge."[5] It is her understanding that "felt-knowledge" isolated to itself is the problem with Protestantism. She writes William Sessions, "When the Protestant hears what he supposes

---

[5]"To Cecil Hawkins," 6 September 1962, *The Habit of Being*, p. 491.

to be the voice of the Lord, he follows it regardless of whether it runs counter to his church's teaching. The Catholic believes any voice he may hear comes from the devil unless it is in accordance with the teachings of the Church."[6] In some instances the voice is the Lord's, she says, as with Old Tarwater in *The Violent Bear It Away*: "his being a Protestant allows him to follow the voice he hears which speaks a truth held by Catholics." In this sense, he is a "natural Catholic." In language more directly anchored in the old distinction between *ratio* and *intellectus*, she writes: "As for the blood and the head business, the blood and the head work together and what is not first in the blood can sometimes reach it [the blood] through the head and what is wrong in the blood can sometimes be tempered by the head."[7] The passage is Thomistic to the core. (Interestingly, she remarks to "A," May 11, 1963, that the sense of comedy is rooted deeply, more deeply than in the head, the *ratio*: "You have to get it in the blood, not in the head.") Flannery O'Connor, as orthodox Christian who practices fiction as an "incarnational" art, is concerned with both the "blood" and the "head" as necessary to her incarnational practice. The artistic difficulty she faces is making palpable through sign and image the complex relation of mind to heart and of both to body and to the body of the world. She does so believing that "A higher paradox confounds emotion as well as reason. . . ."[8]

Given that "higher paradox," we need here to make an important point, lest the seeming separation of *ratio* and *intellectus* be taken to designate a mechanics of mind intolerable to the actual nature of mind as bound in its actions within the paradox. For the naming of these modes is no scholastic species of science's "Sparse and elegant" reductionism. No thinker on this concern is more careful than St. Thomas, the ultimate source of the distinction for Miss O'Connor. He is concerned that

---

[6]"To William Sessions," 29 September 1960, *The Habit of Being*, p. 410.

[7]"To 'A.'," 25 May 1963, *The Habit of Being*, p. 522.

[8]"To 'A.'," 6 September 1955, *The Habit of Being*, p. 100.

analysis of the modes of thought not result in a reductionism whereby *process* of thought is taken to be thought itself. For him, there is always an enveloping mystery in being that speaks a limit to intellectual analysis. With the mind one pursues what St. Thomas calls "the truth of things," but that pursuit does not gain for the mind the ultimate truth. This understood, we remark that our monkish thought about the *ratio* and *intellectus* holds that they are inextricably complementary in the action of the mind, its movement outward beyond what is the particular action of the mind itself. It moves *toward* being which is independent of the action of thought and not to be understood as caused by thought as in those Gnostic elevations of the *ratio* through which the *intellectus* is subordinated or denied. There is being separate from thought, including even the thought upon which one may focus an action of mind.

In modern treatments of the concern, we tend to describe too simply the action of mind as a relation between consciousness and its object, a simplification of the complex "man-thinking" or "mind-thinking." What we intend to speak of here, however, is an engagement that is all one, as it were, an active "relation" of mind to being less divisible than any analysis or description suggests. Since being is a continuous action beyond conceptualization, the "being" of thought itself is so. (This is the problem Thomas engages in his treatise *On Being and Essence*.) Thus we approach a point beyond which full articulation of the action of thought becomes impossible, though having experienced it and reflected upon it we know ourselves to have experienced the action and feel compelled to bear witness. Our witness is that movement of thought whereby we consider, engage, the relation between consciousness and object, an action in itself quite separate from the actuality of thought itself — which actuality the poet attempts beyond the philosopher's handicaps. We may approach it somewhat with the philosopher, and then resign the mystery to the poet, knowing in advance that even the poet will not have comprehended (in a literal sense) the mystery of this action.

The actuality of thought-object, the encounter of the being that is mind with the being not mind, involves an intimacy beyond the powers of articulation, beyond the precisions of verbal formulae. It is a visionary engagement which philosophy arrests by the very act of turning mind upon its own experience. That analytical move, one might say, is out of "science" (philosophy), whereby arrested being is smeared on the transparent slide of finitude and subjected to the scrutiny of analytic reason. But whether smeared on such a slide by the philosophical eye or pinned and wriggling in pentameters by the poet's eye, either specimen of being is already reduced from its complexity. (Hence St. Thomas's reminder of the inadequacy of finite thought to conceptualize being.) The poet, a Wordsworth or Hopkins let us say, struggles to reveal the mystery whereby (in Wordsworth's words) one "sees into the life of things." For Hopkins, the inscape of words and the instress of being meld in a simplicity, though an engagement of that action by words strains inscape and distorts instress. In both the philosopher's and the poet's attempts to bear witness to the mystery of being as witnessed by the actions of thought, he accepts or moves fitfully toward the complementary roles of *ratio* and *intellectus*.

Not to realize the dangers contingent upon separations — of object from thought, of the modes of thought in complement within the complex of thought-object — is to abandon that enveloping larger paradox, against which danger St. Thomas is always staunchly on guard. It is a failure to maintain that guard in Thomistic addresses to being that may even lead to a gnostic use of Thomism itself, against which I spoke earlier. With that warning repeated, we turn more explicitly to the *ratio-intellectus*. Josef Pieper, in his *Leisure: The Basis of Culture*, recalls the distinction, remarking the deconstructive effects upon mind and consequently upon communities of mind when the modes are separated. Here, and in his little book *In Tune with the World: A Theory of Festival*, he illustrates the separation by reference to historical effects out of the separation. He points to such literal

icons of the new idolatry as the statue of Wisdom, declared into
existence by Robespierre. Given our elementary gnostic text
from the college primer quoted earlier — "Society not only
determines what we do but also what we are" — we also need his
reminding us of the formulations by the father of Sociology,
Auguste Comte: among them, Comte's reformed calendar
establishing by dictate "festivals" of Humanity, Paternity,
Domesticity. And Pieper quotes from Rousseau the
fundamentalist tenet of such gnostic adjustments of man and
nature: for the celebration of being as established by the *ratio*
one need only "Plant a flower-decked pole in the middle of an
open place [remember the cleared arenas necessary to modern
gnostic faith], call all the people together — and you have a fête!"

In each of these instances, the presumption is that being is
an effect of the action of mind, that the world is made and
remade by the *ratio*. We are in these instances at a considerable
remove from festival, from significant celebration of being, such
as Pieper poses against these gnostics posturing in being's
presence: *"To celebrate a festival means: to live out, for some
special occasion and in an uncommon manner, the universal assent
to the world as a whole."* (His italics.) That is to be in tune with
the world, rather than assuming oneself the world's manipulator.
The "things" of festival are thereby made votive, lifted up; in
David Jones's words, "in whatever manner made over to the
gods." (The nature of festival is the central theme of Jones's
Anathemata, as its title indicates, and his preface to that great
poem is very much supportive of our position.) The gnostic
festival, to the contrary, treats things, including persons,
arbitrarily to the convenience of the intellect which has
disengaged itself from existence.

Turning from Rousseau's "fête" to a gnostic one of our own,
we may notice in it a struggle underway to recover the older and
valid sense of festival. Recall the elaborate celebrations of the
rededication of the Statue of Liberty (July 1986), the attempt to
raise votive voices in unison to "liberty," an abstraction divorced

of the complexities of being at the level of both person and community of persons. Excessive spectacle in the event did not hide the accompanying pathos, a recognition out of the heart — the *intellectus* — that somehow the festival was incomplete. Those works cited earlier — Voegelin, Jaki, *et al.* — which examine the ways whereby mind has been untuned from the world by post-Renaissance thought — cast light on why neither our leisure nor our festival reflect a satisfying relation of man to existence. And through those works, we might better understand the sense of incompleteness that accompanied our national attempt at rededication to "liberty." We were largely left with spectacle, the ghost of action, rather than a sense of having participated in significant action. We recall that it is the ghost of action, rather than the actuality of action, that is the agitating state of Flannery O'Connor's characters, representations of that disoriented address to existence that results when nature is cut off from grace by the gnostic mind. That is the popular spirit of the 1980s, focused for a moment in the glare of fireworks over the New York harbor, fading into a dark silence in the national spirit.

ix

In the 1920s T.S. Eliot suggested that we have experienced "a dissociation of sensibility," a separation of thought and feeling, and he suggests that separation fostered by Milton and Dryden. A poet like John Donne, to the contrary, caught a "direct sensuous apprehension of thought" in words. Eliot's seems largely a matter of literary concern, profitable to critical minds treating the texts of poems — some reflecting the dominance of "thought," some of "feeling." A mode may dominate a whole literary period, and thus we juxtapose the Age of Reason to the Romantic Age. But it began to dawn upon the intellectual community, especially after World War II, that the antipathy of these modes of sensibility affects the very fabric of society, as a consequence of a civil war within that intellectual community. Something more than literary criticism seems at issue. Hence that spirited debate, in and out of the academy, sparked by C.P. Snow's lament that we are now divided into "two cultures," the one dominated by scientific thought, the other by humanistic thought. On which side lies merely the ghost of intellectual action, as opposed to significant action of the mind — on science's or on the humanities'? Which faction shall lead us to the promised land of social order? Is feeling the villain, or thought?

When we reflect on the problem, we realize that the factions here set against each other were long since established in antipathetic roles in the academy itself, in schools of "Arts and Sciences." But we have already urged that the separation, rising to a popular concern following Snow's *Two Cultures*, antedates our own Age of Alienation, as well as the Romantic Age and the

Age of Reason. It antedates even Occam, being a division of mind established by ancient Gnostic thought. If this division in intellectual modes is always with us, if in that division we are cut off from the fullness of our being, both mediately and ultimately robbed of our *status viatoris* and denied thereby the hope of *status comprehensoris*, it becomes something more than a problem of antiquarian interest, a problem in "the history of ideas." For the confusions attendant to the dislocations affect us in the ground of our individual and community existence at this very moment. Modern gnosticism, then, is a term naming a climate of thought daily breathed, deleterious to mind's and spirit's healthful relation to reality, contributing to our vaporization as persons. It must be dealt with, with the recognition that its confusions have developed exponentially since the concerted introduction of Nominalism into Western thought.

What modern gnosticism has accomplished to our general confusion is the establishment of the *ratio* over the *intellectus*. The two modes, always threatening opposition within an individual mind or community of minds, had its decisive context established for intellectual civil war by Nominalism. For Nominalism usurped language itself as the instrument with which to pry mind loose from creation, declaring "names" arbitrary. Richard Weaver, in *Ideas Have Consequences* (a book which Miss O'Connor read), remarks the dislocation:

> Logic became grammaticized, passing from a science which taught men *vere loqui* to one which taught *recte loqui* or from an ontological division by categories to a study of signification, with the inevitable focus upon historical meanings. [A meaning established as historical is easily rejected, as Mrs. Lucynell Crater shows us: the monks of old are not as advanced as we are.] Here begins the assault upon definition: if words no longer correspond to objective

realities, it seems no great wrong to take liberties with words.[1]

We acknowledge, at least tacitly in our historical labels, the separation of mind from reality, along with the accompanying struggle between *ratio* and *intellectus*, a struggle within the mind for control of its language. We speak of "The Age of Reason," followed by "The Romantic Age," titles supporting considerable specialized industries in the academy in this century. But our concern over these separations becomes of more than literary or antiquarian interest when we see the consequences in our present actions in the world. It dawns slowly and disturbingly upon us that perhaps those dislocations radically affect our being, complicate our moment-to-moment encounter with reality.

One engages the history of this development, then, not to arrest history and catalogue the past, but to learn to recognize in the present moment inherited carcinogenic ideas lodged in the mind. Thus one looks the more closely at Descartes's desperate attempt to certify his own mind, at Bacon's principle that "Knowledge is power." One looks the more cautiously at Hume and Hegel and Kant and Leibniz. One hears Kierkegaard's passionate alarm sounded against the mind's deconstructions of reality. And one opposes the more firmly his late listener, Sartre, who seizes upon the *ratio*'s advantage in a grammatized logic to establish dogmatically the primacy of self. That Sartrean ferocity of words divorced from reality would establish mind as monad, as the sole universe. So it becomes a matter of community survival no less than of personal survival to oppose such radical deconstructions of reality, wherever they confront us.

The deconstructions of reality practiced by Sartre have, in a line of descent from Nominalism, a "literary" offspring now dying but not without continuing destructions of mind that will be some years with us. I have in mind the new criticism called

---

[1]Richard Weaver, *Ideas Have Consequences* (Chicago: University of Chicago Press, 1948), p. 7.

"deconstruction," spawned by Saussure, whose principal disciple is Derrida. The destruction of mind involved in their ideology continues because the academy, in the interest of providing its students with the very latest, is blinded to the ancient gnostic nature of this seemingly new deconstruction. It has therefore willingly imported the latest French idea, *via* Yale, into its curriculum, largely for the aura of its being French in origin and mediated by Yale. Its most immediate parentage is Nihilistic Existentialism, its more proximate origin Nominalism, as is clear from Saussure's principles. His opening axiom, to be taken without any firm examination, is "*the principle of the arbitrary nature of the sign*," an obvious derivative of Occam. Dismissing out of mind the common sense understanding of language as an attempt to name actualities independent of the naming mind, Saussure declares a "*principle of the rational nature of all linguistic meaning.*"[2] Thus, in Saussure's own words, the sign — the word — unites "not a thing and name, but a concept and a sound-image." The effect of this second principle is to radically sever mind unto itself, excluding anything not mind but declaring in a mystery inaccessible to the uninitiated that language is the matrix in which is suspended pre-existing idea, summoned into a presence (*vide* Heidegger) in consciousness by the rational nature of linguistic meaning. There is here no acknowledgement of linguistic meaning as attached to any reality separate from the consciousness; consciousness is thus conceived in isolation from reality and enclosed by the hermetic fiat that language is internal to consciousness.

There are differences played out by various deconstructionists, Derrida himself bouncing off Saussure's "text" to perform his own acrobatics. In doing so, he is required to reject that text as existing in the reality of another mind, though not clearly acknowledging that requirement as dictated by the

---

[2]These last quoted words are a summary of Saussure advanced by Colin Falck in his "Saussurian Theory and the Abolition of Reality," *The Monist*, January 1986: 133-145.

Saussurian principles. The position that reveals the fundamental fallacy in deconstruction is summarized by Falck in the essay cited: "From the idea that words do not have their meanings by virtue of their one-to-one correspondences with items in reality, it is inferred *tout court* that language cannot be held to relate in an intelligible or usefully discussable way with any extra-linguistic dimension or 'presence' in reality at all." What this means is that, since Saussure's argument is produced out of the mouth of a creature existing in an "extra-linguistic dimension" (does a Derrida send copies of his game words to Saussure, expect words in return, talk to students at Yale?), the language used by Derrida, seemingly in response to language used (i.e., "published") by Saussure, has no point of contact on principle with Saussure.

We are dealing with a radical solipsism which is at every point self-contradictory, a fear that leads Derrida to an absurdity: "Perception is precisely a concept, a concept of an intuition or of a given originating from the thing itself, present itself in its meaning, independently from language, from the system of references." By defining perception as concept, while attempting to disengage both idea and language from any reality separate from consciousness, Derrida nevertheless makes tacit admission of existence separate from the closed world of "signifier" (called "Derrida") and "signified," the namer and the name — not, we must note carefully, the *named*, which may not be admitted to exist under penalty of the collapse of deconstruction. A tenuous connection of consciousness to anything beyond its closed world is hinted at in "intuition," which is itself presumably an aspect of consciousness but one susceptible to the temptation of the demiurge — i.e., existence that is not the consciousness. That temptation leads to perception — to an acknowledgement of external existence without which perception could not be. For perception alone may answer the tempted "intuition." Such statement endangers the whole deconstructionist position, as Derrida realizes, and so he adds the absurdity: "I don't believe there is any perception." Thus we have public announcement of dogma out of what can only be described as an act of faith that perception does not exist. But to whom is the definition and its negation addressed? If consistent to principle, only to Derrida. Yet the words appear in *The Structuralist Controversy*[3], following their pronouncement in a public gathering of minds. At a more homely level, since perception is beyond Derrida's belief, one wonders with what confidence he orders steak or wine. Whether he sends essays and books to editors or cashes royalty checks?

What is very deliberately rejected by deconstruction (and in that rejection is revealed a deliberate gnostic act) is, in Falck's devastating critique, "the dimension of what once used to be called our *religious awareness.* . . . What Saussurian theory offers us, with its elimination from our lives of incarnation, transcendence, the self, intuition, creativity, apprehended extra-linguistic meaning, determinable textual meaning (if there is no 'presence,' then all textual readings are veridically equal), poetry (if there is no 'naming,' then all readings are poetically equal), historical context, and truth, is the Abolition of Reality."

If this is indeed what deconstruction offers — as I believe it to be — the baffling question is why this "movement" has been so welcomed by the academy. I have already suggested one reason: academics are as susceptible to intellectual fads as their students to dress. An additional reason is that, given the recent history of the teacher of philosophy and literature within the academy — the necessity of establishing reputation through published words — deconstruction was doubly welcomed: by the professor, since Shakespeare's use of images is long since exhausted by scholarly publication; by the academic powers, since they are ravenous for newfangledness, given their loss of vision as to the role the academy plays or should play in society.

Indeed, *play* is a most suitable term in relation to deconstruction. On the one hand, the academic deconstruction-

---

[3](Baltimore: Johns Hopkins University Press, 1972).

ist is faced with the problem of teaching functional illiterates to write job applications (of one sort or another). On the other, he must establish a "speciality" in a world where more traditional "specialists" abound. What could be a more inviolate speciality than deconstruction, since it depends on principles of absolute relativity which academic administrators from department heads to deans are generally incompetent to expose. Why incompetent?

Well, given the excited attention to deconstruction in France (where the movement is now largely dead) a certain validity is granted by the intellectual community without an examination. The movement itself declares as dogma that language is both disembodied in itself and without any context separate from the isolated deconstructionist's mind within which it is said to be suspended; the saying is the only proof demanded. Having no relation to existence separate from that mind, one must (if he is perhaps an academic dean) depend on the assurance by that mind that such an address to language is intellectually valid. One is subsequently given a species of progress report (if one is a dean), from the mind-lab. Who would be so gauche as to question intellectual freedom in such pursuits? To do so would be to demonstrate oneself anti-intellectual, which is academic blasphemy. One must then be content with his "layman's" response to this new science and its practitioner.

Meanwhile, the games begin, the uninitiated watching with the disquiet supposed to affect the bourgeois mind when it encounters the latest blow-torch sculpture. Indeed, let the games begin! With the cry "the author is dead" (the deconstructionist's adaptation of Nietzsche), words are stripped of both their present and their past, if such stripping is in the interest of the game afoot. A still moment of the gnostic mind is declared into existence, within which the new critic works his will, an alchemy to which only he has pure access and of which magical effect he only is therefore adequate judge. The base is turned gold — we are told. He uses a "text" as a trampoline upon which to perform

private imaginative gyrations. The text is inconsequential. One
has a private exhibitionism at public expense and indulgence, but
beyond the public's participation. Another deconstructionist may
use the same text, a further contradiction of the deliberate
exclusion of reality, since texts are accepted, presumably by
"intuition" as existing separate from mind. But his performance is
quite independent, since he performs his own figures. It is the
performance alone that matters, though accessible only to the
performer. Even so, the "notes" of his score are published, since
through such certifications of external reality, more real than
intuitional, come monies that allow one to move up from
hamburger to steak — medium or more probably rare.

One might tolerate such exhibitionism — some of it is in
fact intellectually entertaining, not without wit. But then one is
confronted by serious argument justifying its intellectual validity.
Argument is required since after all, summer grants and research
time are desired. The performance is made possible by public
support, a perception rather more immediately encroaching upon
the purity of the isolated mind than Derrida acknowledges. It is
at the point of serious defense of deconstruction that the shell
game is exposed: credos become automatically contradictory of
the articles of deconstructionist faith. For instance, when the
deconstructionist insists that language is infinite, without rational
limitations and so a given text suited to infinite readings, the
defensive argument itself assumes the contrary. The words
advancing the position in order to justify deconstruction can do
so only if they have finite, discrete meaning.

Deconstruction turns out to be a species of Dadaism, now
given academic respectability and granted the same serious
curiosity Gulliver exhibits toward the Academy of Laputa. Like
Dada, it is a fad, though alas not a passing fad since species of
exhibitionist anarchy surface in any culture when that culture
finds itself under severe pressure to discover and maintain
intellectual and spiritual order. As a moment of distraction to
relax severe intellectual tension, it has its moments — as does an

occasional situation comedy on television. As a theory of criticism, as an address to the nature of language in relation to mind and thus to be studied with an academic seriousness, it is at once ludicrous and dangerous: ludicrous since it pretends that nonsense is sense, dangerous since it subverts the order of mind in community when the stewards of the orderly mind — professors of philosophy and history and literature — have lost the authority of mind necessary to their stewardship — though Ph.Ds. abound.

X

There would seem to be a sufficiently pressing need for the recovery of the scholastic modes of thought, whatever name we might give them, since under a variety of names we speak of a reality in our experience of thought in the world. The scholastic argument holds that, through the *intellectus*, the mind is encouraged to a concern for the truth of things. The *intellectus*, by analogy, responds to being as the eye to a landscape, seeking detail and panoramic view. It is a pull in us to see a thing both particularly and wholly — that is, in its relation to the wholeness of existence. It is the mode of the *intellectus* that prompts Flannery O'Connor to remark that "The longer you look at one object, the more of the world you see in it." It is also, more anciently, the mode Heraclitus characterizes as a "listening to the essence of things." It is the balancing mode in a view of existence we associate with the heart, as we associate the *ratio* with the head. The distinction, then, is both ancient and contemporary, not depending necessarily upon intellectual tradition for its survival, since we are likely to discover it for ourselves when at moments we are in tune with the world. We do find the distinction in the formal language of both poet and philosopher, as well as at the level of common, everyday discourse. ("I don't know where my mind was!" Or, "He has no heart.")

It is in Homer and Aeschylus. In Virgil and Dante, Milton and Wordsworth, Eliot and Frost — names touched randomly to suggest intellectual continuity; it is a present presence Eliot calls tradition. The poet speaks of it figuratively or dramatizes it. Thus the characterization of Clytaemnestra in the opening speech of the *Agamemnon*: she is in outer appearance a woman, "but her heart is as stout as ever a man's," whereby we are to understand that Clytaemnestra gives a public display to the heart — her womanly nature — but only to mask her resolute intent to act vengefully against Agamemnon in what she defends as a reasonable action in the name of justice. Her action is through the dictates of the *ratio*, to apply our terms. The presence of the *intellectus* is poignant in Virgil's lament for "the tears of things." Closer to us, the separation of the *ratio* and the *intellectus* in Eliot's Prufrock establishes the tensional poles of that famous character. (Before resolving the dramatic necessities, Eliot wrote two dialogues between the body and soul, unpublished but surviving in manuscript.) The immediate speaking voice of "The Love Song of J. Alfred Prufrock" *knows* all, descending toward nothingness in despair, while yet resisting the *you's* pull toward the created world. And it is Eliot's recognition of the complementary nature of the *ratio* and *intellectus* that prompts him to use a passage from the *Agamemnon* as epigraph to "Sweeney Among the Nightingales," a poem in which the dissociation of sensibility is the central theme.

One finds a similar disjunction of *ratio* and *intellectus* as the dominant theme in the poetry of Robert Frost, dramatized in the encounters between men and women, given local incarnation by New England language, landscape, and history. It is in "West-Running Brook," "The Death of the Hired Man," "Home Burial." The disjunction is internalized in a single speaker in many lyrics: "Mending Wall," "Stopping by a Woods," "The Road Not Taken," and very overtly expressed in "On the Heart's Beginning to Cloud the Mind." For Frost, the game between mind and heart "makes" the consciousness — an Existentialist dimension in him. But his is a private emphasis as opposed to the Puritan public contest with nature. Where Winthrop is dedicated to a shining city on a hill as a bastion against and a refutation of the satanic wilderness, Frost is content to establish his poem as a "momentary stay against confusion" at a more private level. That address, of course, always requires a new poem in the next moment. Late in life, Frost rejects Emerson as a "cheerful Monist," saying that for himself a "melancholy dualism is the only soundness." He adds a haunting acknowledgment of his own spiritual dislocation, "the question is: is soundness [i.e., intellectual soundness on the point] of the essence."

The drama of Frost's poetry is an interior one, though he is marvelously accomplished at giving an incarnational presence to interior conflict through character, imagery, and idiom. One may read the corpus of Frost's work most satisfactorily, I believe, under his own repeated metaphor of the game. That game consists of mind valued by him though not, I believe, understood by him, and certainly not in the scholastic manner we propose, in consequence of which he is at last inescapably a gnostic, the dualism from his point of view a game between *pneuma* and *psyche*. Nature he projects as inhabited by demiurge. Hence the melancholy of his dualism. That pull toward creation we have called the mode of the *intellectus*, the "heart." He calls it a pull of the heart as well, but he sees it as a pull toward oblivion, a pull to woods that are "lovely, dark and deep." This demiurgic summoning to oblivion he is never quite ready to conclude diabolic, since in a resistance by the *ratio* (the head) he posits a necessary second pole; between head and heart lies the arena within which one comes to be. Frost's view of the woods, then, makes interesting contrast when juxtaposed to Miss O'Connor's and reveals a strain of romantic pathos in Frost which he works very hard to control by the *ratio*. For he is almost as fearful of the "Romanticism" he senses in himself as is James Joyce. To that fearfulness, one suspects, we owe the very playfulness in Frost to which we most warmly respond, not noticing very much the dark melancholic depth. His work, we conclude, sustains a serious play against the dark pull, and with a skill that hides the darkness from the casual eye. One might, however, read "Home-Burial" as the dark underside of "The Death of the Hired Man," and from there discover that there is a dark undersurface crucial to the dramatic effectiveness of "The Death of the Hired Man" itself.

If Frost is a more popular poet than Eliot, one might suppose it because, although he gives artful incarnation to a theme common to both, he does so with more familiar imagery, out of a more familiar history because it is a history adjacent to our personal memory, as a broader Western intellectual history is not. That is, Frost is less given to ranging after the causes of the dissociation of sensibility than Eliot. Which is not to say that Frost is unaware of much of the ground Eliot explores. Frost, too, is a "classicist" in literature, though his classicism is not so conspicuous in his poetry as is Eliot's. Frost, like Eliot, is aware of Bergson's attempt to overthrow mechanistic science. While Eliot is explicit about his being drawn to those ancient minds that contend with modern problems — Heraclitus, Aeschylus, Plato, Aristotle — Frost is rather content to learn a lesson as poet from Homer and Virgil, from the *Odyssey* and the *Georgics*. We note his approach to Virgil in contrast to Eliot's — through the pastorals rather than through Dante's view of the *Aeneid* and Dante's concern for an earthly city in relation to the Heavenly City. Frost is not above being caustically and pettily derisive of Eliot, not simply because of Eliot's heavily literary adaptations but I believe because of Eliot's Christian emphasis. Whatever the cause, Frost is caustic to an extent that he seems rather anti-intellectual. This is a stance assumed to curry favor with the popular mind, one suspects, a public disquieted by Eliot's "learning." There is, then, not only a dark side but a reprehensible side to Frost. But his unfortunate jealousies aside, he is more "learned" than he lets on, that learning surfacing in his poetry. He touches upon his own version of a dissociation of disbelief, for instance, finding the cause in the ancient contentions between Democritus and Plato, though he puts the point whimsically. Man as "The Bear" is caught "Between two metaphysical extremes," restless in his cage. In his restlessness he "almost looks religious but he's not." His worshipful gestures are only in fact his sitting back "on his fundamental butt," swaying his snout from side to side,

At one extreme agreeing with one Greek.
At the other agreeing with another Greek. . . .

Except for the whimsy, one might suspect a bitterness toward man in Frost akin to that we attribute to Swift. Our purpose here has been to suggest how constant and widespread in history and in history's continuing social body is this recognition of the "dissociation of sensibility," this separation of modes of thought into warring *ratio* and *intellectus* as we are contending. Poets seemingly diverse and antipathetic reflect the concern if we but look closely: Milton and Pope; Wordsworth and Keats; and in our current illustration, Eliot and Frost. Eliot and Frost each engage the poles of thought and feeling, *ratio* and *intellectus*, seeing them in conflict with each other in the modern mind; each sees in some degree the origin of the conflict as lying in the intellectual movements of Western history. We might add that the dissociation of these modes of mind is also widely recognized in the popular mind. It is, for instance, the stock traded upon in gospel and country music. (One may supply illustration from his own acquaintance with popular art other than gospel or country music.) In gospel music one meets the Puritan gnostic, whereas country music, now preempted by the Nashville entrepreneur, has very rapidly become a country of secular gnosticism, so sharply at odds with gospel music that it is most strange that open war has not been developed between them, as there has between Fundamentalist gospel patrons and Hard Rock. In both gospel and country songs the metaphor of the conflict of heart and head is tediously repeated, heart leading the one sentimentally to Heaven, the other sentimentally into hedonism.

Given these recognitions, we may now say something of the "signs" used to talk about the dissociation, the images through which attempts are made at reconciliation. For it is simply foolish to suggest that in the range of literature we have touched upon, from Homer to country music, the interest is only in a relation between the *namer* and the *name*. The question of the *named* is always to the fore, and a concern for a satisfying commerce between the namer and the named, for which the name itself is assumed a mediator more or less effective. The conflict between *ratio* and *intellectus* as revealed in the struggle to make names effective, especially in relation to the literature of that struggle, tends to find a common center for art's incarnational task: sex, the universal clue to the mystery of existence — from *Genesis* to television's situation comedy. Which leads me to suggest that it is "love" that is the necessary catalyst to the reunification of the modes of thought which we see so variously pursued. This is a most ancient observation, of course, but one that needs most special attention as we witness the collapse of social community about us. At the popular level of the concern, there is the tedious variety of battles of the sexes, given comic treatment in television's "sitcoms" but a quite different treatment in the alarming studies of the disintegration of the family and preponderance of births to unwed teenagers and the growing confusion in society itself such as those centering on "single-parent households" — a term that smacks of gnostic analysis. See the definitions of *home* in Frost's "Death of the Hired Man."

In those literary works, classical and popular, that survive and to which we return again and again, one finds a resonance beyond the sexual at an animal level. Odysseus, at no loss for sexual comforts on his long wandering, yet recalls not just Penelope as woman, but the climate of love binding them for which he has rejected Calypso's proffer of eternal youth with her on an island paradise. Later, standing naked, reduced almost to death, before the Princess Nausicaa, he prays for her such a love as his, if she will help him: a marriage in which she will have with her husband "a mind at one with his . . . a good gift, for there is nothing mightier and nobler than when man and wife are of one heart and mind in a house, a grief to their foes, and to their friends great joy, but their own hearts know it best." The natural manifestation of love — at times comic, sentimental, tragic — suggests something larger enclosing the love, even in its most pagan setting. In this light we remember Macbeth and his Lady no less than Tristan and Iseult. For in a resonant literary work, we repeat, love moves inexorably beyond the physical act upon which pornography is intent in its frantic pursuit of variation in the love act itself. What lies deep in artful love is the pursuit of an ordinate love of all being; that is the common well-spring of significant art. There is an abiding truth, then, in sentimental cliché, and if we are uncomfortable with the cliché, one trusts it is because one at least knows a difference between sentiment and sentimentality. The cliché: all the world loves a lover; the lover in love loves all the world. The ordinate love of existence, then, is art's one and inescapable theme, the ordinate pursuit itself yielding the varieties of pathos, comedy, tragedy. Remembering Andrew Lytle's remark that the opposite of love is not hate but power, we recognize love and its perversions in all great literature: *The Agamemnon, Medea, The Divine Comedy, Macbeth, War and Peace, The Brothers Karamazov.*

In literary works there is an added "body," as it were, when the common theme is anchored in sexual agents. (The "sexual" problem with Lady Macbeth has been a very popular critical topic.) Love in relation to procreation is the firmest anchor of art, given the waste of generation we experience in the world as we are "on the way," in our hunger for fulfillment. The sexual act seems at once promising and inadequate, giving rise to the temptation of power as antidote to our failed love. Not that literal sexual love need be the point of departure in the quest for love. The violent pursuit of ordinate love, a love at once recognized and denied, is the theme of Flannery O'Connor's *The Violent Bear It Away.* Her Rayber is terrified by a love he can only explain as a madness inherited through his blood, a madness that threatens him at any moment he allows his attention to rest on any object in existence separate from his own mind. From an orthodox position, Rayber's should be a welcomed madness whose necessity is out of that old complicity in the Garden of Eden over the question of power, in a context which carries sexual overtones. A love restored is in the offing for Rayber, a healing of Original Sin, but he can understand the offering only as an effect of degenerate genes in the long orgy of procreation, a condition of nature which only his rational mind can heal.

Having turned his world upside down with his reason, he cannot distinguish effect from enveloping cause. That he should be seized by such a seeming perversion of love that turns him toward objects of nature is the source of a confused terror before which his reason is helpless. "It could be a stick or stone, the line of a shadow, the absurd old man's walk of a starling." What happens to Rayber in such moments is "a morbid surge of love . . . powerful enough to throw him to the ground in an act of idiot praise. It was completely irrational and abnormal." Irrational to Rayber, whose consent to any worship at all is restricted by his will so that it centers on the rational dimension of his own being. No wonder Miss O'Connor is puzzled by responses, even sympathetic responses, that miss this point. She says to "A," "You say there is love between man and God in the stories, but never between people — yet the grandmother is not the least concerned with God but reaches out to touch the Misfit. . . . Rayber's love for Bishop is the purest love I have ever dealt with. It is because of its terrifying purity that Rayber has to destroy it."[1]

Our inadequacy in coming to terms with the terrifying purity possible to love is the most damaging bequest to us from secular gnosticism, leading us from *caritas* to Community Chest. The history of mind's subversion of love is worth long analysis and meditation, but I shall touch upon it only by recalling Karl Stern's exploration of the psychological and philosophical disjunctions of love in the modern mind. In his *Flight from Woman*,[2] Stern considers the dissociation of sensibilities in such post-

---

[1]"To 'A.,'" 5 March 1960, *The Habit of Being*, p. 379.

[2]Karl Stern, *The Flight from Woman* (New York: Farrar, Straus, and Giroux, 1965).

Renaissance figures as Descartes, Schopenhauer, Kierkegaard, Tolstoy, Goethe, Freud, and others. He does so by a comparison of the thought bequeathed us by these minds as that thought appears in its historical context, specifically within the texture of the men's personal lives. What interests Stern in his study is the conflict in these men's thought as underlined by their personal difficulties in establishing an ordinate love of creation, most usually a love centering on particular women. In his words, he observes that "'intellect' and 'heart' stand in antithesis, and that the 'heart' is linked to the feminine." The "heart" or "intuition" binds mind to being, an uncomfortable tie, given what we have described as the gnostic inclination prompted by the *ratio* enslaved by will. The terror Rayber experiences is a very real one to a Descartes or a Kierkegaard, for instance. On this point, Stern (a practicing psychiatrist) observes that "When we get to know patients who experience the panic which Kierkegaard experienced with Regina [Olsen] we observe, phenomenologically and apart from all psychological significance, something which is best described as *terror of the irreversible* or *terror of the commitment*, which is closely related to the fear of death."[3] The point is the more arresting as we remember that Kierkegaard's terror occurs when Regina consents to marry him. We are reminded of the absence of such terror in a Dante or a Yeats, for whom Beatrice and Maude Gonne are inaccessible in the world, where the poets are *homo viator*. Stern's remark also casts considerable light on Prufrock, and on O'Connor's Rayber and Haze Motes as well.

The "fear of death" of which Stern speaks is related at least analogically to that of Saul on the Road to Damascus. Stern knows this, since he is not only a practicing psychiatrist but an orthodox Christian. It is Saul become Paul who speaks again and again of that death as necessary. He had marched against it in terror till blinded by revelation. It is the death of the old man

---

[3]Karl Stern, *The Flight from Woman*, p. 225.

that the new may be "put on." One meets the same complex of fear dramatized in a "flight from woman" in Eliot's poetry, which Eliot reconciled at last to the created world in *Little Gidding*. Flannery O'Connor presents it through her Saul, Haze Motes. Indeed, Haze is in some instances most comically shown in "flight from woman," his aggressive indifference to Leora Watts a forced confrontation to prove there is no flight. He "persecutes" creation, most explicitly his own body when he drives it to the edge of physical collapse. (We have indicated already that the expiation he undertakes at the novel's end is of another order.) Such are the concerns Karl Stern explores in his chosen philosophers and poets, his central point being that agonies of mind stem from immediate engagements with a world separate from mind. The agony is consequence of a refusal of that love, to which one is invited through the immediate and actual existence of the world. The resulting agony is stilled only when we learn to love creation aright.

What I am suggesting, by reference to both fictional and actual persons who have borne witness to this struggle with a terror in the presence of creation, is that the mode in our intellect which the scholastics called *intellectus* and we call *heart* holds us in orbit to the existential world, against dislocations possible when we deny all existence save the *ratio*, the *head*. The *ratio*, freed of that centripetal pull into nature and toward the Cause of being which is to be discovered through nature, would reject all being out of a "terror of death" of the self. In the violence of its centrifugal escape into a closed vacuum of mind once *intellectus* is dislodged, it establishes *idea* to be worshipped as the only reality, as the only escape possible from the complexities of finitude. But the center of finitude, inescapably, is the very self that wills an escape from its own being. Little wonder that, in an age largely dominated by such attempts, we call the age alienated and its spiritual climate that of *angst*. Nor should it be of wonder to us that, when love is perverted in the interest of power, the social world falls apart. It falls outward, as we are daily reminded in the media, from that central focal point of love in the social world, the family. The body, ordained by Love for a social fulfillment, is in collapse because of the gnostic desire for power over being, whether the being of the Beloved or that of one's children. When personhood is reduced to animal nature, out of which reduction a power is commanded against both it and creation in general, not only the person but the sacral order of a person's existence is destroyed. Here is the repeated blow that is destroying family.

xi

Not that the *intellectus* is completely ignored in modern thought. That pull in our being is still sufficiently insistent that it can't be completely ignored any more than the ancient Gnostic could, whose solution was to associate it with the *psyche* as internal surrogate of the world's demiurge. Even Derrida speaks of an "instinct" that gives rise to a "concept" that is so near perception as to require his denying that perception exists. There is likewise a modified hint of it in Freudianism. If we call it "instinct" (one of its more popular names) or the *id* (now less popular than thirty years ago), we may relegate it to a presence in our animal nature, a presence not yet surmounted by the evolutionary perfection of our accidental being. Thus through the agency of will to restructure our being, we may move toward fulfillment. Of course, since the will must itself have anchor in animal nature, what we in effect anticipate is a lifting of ourselves by our bootstraps. With such a presumption, the way seems open nevertheless to a final removal of this unwanted presence in the mind by the surgical skills of the *ratio*, powered by will. We shall then be reborn, capable of flights beyond biological matter. That failing, we shall at least subjugate the idiot *id* through psychoanalysis — yoke animal impulse. Such is the flight suggested by our uneasiness that Stern speaks of. Figuratively at least, the problem is a "flight from woman."

But what I am saying is that this flight is one away from the complexity of the very thing that is in flight. It is a flight from parts or the whole of creation with which modern rationality seems most uncomfortable. Creation is thus cast as antagonist. In that action of flight we only dramatize, and hide by the dramatizing, a central truth: the flight is from ourselves, from the self we must learn to love ordinately in all its complexity so that we may then come to love all existence. It is through that love that we enter the Mercy of Love, which is one of the names of the paradox enclosing our thought and feeling in the intricacy of a living being we speak of as our self. The one determination of being is that first and last Being, in whose image the self is made. One reads works like Pieper's *In Tune with the World* and *On Hope* to understand the flight from "woman" to be a flight into hopelessness, mind and soul destined to be buffeted by despair.

It becomes something of a dilemma for the fugitive *ratio*, intent on rejecting the present ground of its own being, when it must reconsider recent advanced studies of the mind.   Such studies would surely impress a Mrs. Lucynell Crater, who can take in stride Mr. Shiftlet's indictment of "one of these doctors in Atlanta that's taken a knife and cut the human heart . . . out of a man's chest and held it in his hand . . . and studied it like it was a day-old chicken. . . ." The *intellectus* will not so easily yield to such indifference, however, for that lingering, dejected resident (the *intellectus*) in consciousness appears intimate to the body, a part of its actual being, its incorporation, as well as agent in that continuing incorporation — our coming-to-be. But now the *ratio* appears as intimately related to our body, beyond a division that would elevate it. Current physiological science pursues each into the physical brain itself. If one had hoped to exorcise "instinct" from the body, it now seems that to do so requires an isolation of the right hemisphere, perhaps even its neutralization. Even so, the latest laboratory study suggests that the brain's hemispheres are not to be separated in their functions so easily as recently supposed: the right hemisphere also participates in language actions, the left in visual and spatial tasks — a complication of the earlier suppositions about the hemispheres' separated roles in mind's actions.[1]   To separate "thought" (language and

---

[1]See *Science News*, 2 August 1986.

perception) into discrete geographies of the brain becomes problematic, just as the logical separation of the *ratio* and *intellectus* would be.

Short of the extreme measure of lobotomy, perhaps one might be content to employ the "libido" in the "ego's" amusement through a primitive Freudian "science" now being rapidly superseded by biochemistry. One might do so, cultivating an indifference to it which yet allows to the mythical Ego a superiority to biological origins, the only origin allowed by modern gnosticism. What happens when such a confused address to being is made in the name of sciences and pseudo-sciences? Perhaps the answer is in the spectacle of encounter currently much in the news, though seemingly far removed from the physiology of the brain, the public brawl over pornography. The spectacle in the public arena involves several species of gnostics, intellects detached in one way or another from complex reality — Puritan, secular, chauvinist, feminist. Names fly thickly, the factions divisible, though compassed in gnostic vapors.

The response by the intellectual community to the two-volume Meese Commission report on pornography (July 1986) is very confusing. At points, outrage against the report centers on "Constitutional" issues with a fervor for term and logic not unlike our popular version of the scholastic's pursuits of angels on pinheads. Official or semi-official (the latter largely media columnists) declare an apocalyptic end to our cherished freedoms, if we prove so foolish as to grant judicial leverage against pornography. At another level, the question of whether a demonstrable relation exists between the "art" of pornography and acts of sexual violence in community is debated with refinements that remind one more of the Sophists than of the Scholastics. But these new freedom-fighters find themselves handicapped by their own old arguments, making sophistry almost a necessity. Those old arguments have now been institutionalized in, for instance, the National Endowment for the Arts, whose existence depends upon a faith that art does indeed affect the social body. From the days of the Marxist 1930s through the Age of the Holy Innocents (the 1960s), the conviction grew that art does in fact and ought as an institutionalized program affect society. But now there is the necessity assumed in the same quarters to dissociate art as affecting society, given the movement against pornography. The accumulation of psychological, biological data, the statistics from hospitals and police dealings with violence, etc., etc., require banks of computers to turn data into ammunition to be used in this new freedom fight, so multitudinous is the evidence.

If the well-being of persons and the community of persons were not at risk, rather than merely the vaporous ideas about ideological "freedoms" and "liberties," one might be content to watch the comic activities in the public arena that accompany our moral and intellectual bankruptcy, ourselves safely protected by irony. There is something of the desperate splurge about the affair, as if recognizing "instinctively" reality's pending foreclosure. But the consequences are too grave for a detached irony, though we may at least wonder whether we aren't witnessing a morality play, a "happening" of more epic proportion than those notorious ones of the 1960s. Or perhaps it is elegiac only, this dying fall we might call "Gnostics in Gehenna; or, The Promised Land Besieged."

Stanley L. Jaki, in a quiet analysis of our intellectual bankruptcy as evidenced in neo-Darwinism, remarks, "Gehenna is merely the ultimate and eternal form of anarchy. This is to be kept in mind when humanist Darwinists, including most college professors, are reminded by a fellow academic of the rank inconsistency of their references to moral norms as they recommend, say, the ethical stance of civil disobedience in fighting against racial inequality." Father Jaki's point is that one can't have it both ways. One can't establish as a religious tenet of secular faith that whatever is is an inevitable consequence of evolutionary survivals, the only reality, and then propose a moral concern which contradicts the Darwinian theology. (Father Jaki, obviously, opposes racial inequality, but on grounds other than Darwinian.) His point applies most directly to the question of pornography, in that if man is a creature determined by his genes under the pressure of the moment's environment, to oppose the opposers of pornography cannot be undertaken seriously. It is as unreasonable as the finite argument of deconstructionists that language is infinite. The gnostic defenders of freedom, if one may judge from their moral tenets, are engaged at most in a game played to while away the emptiness of time. Deterministic biology, accompanied by whatever flowering of pornography or high love (each equally acceptable from deterministic principle), will work its way. One might as well see it a comic game, as such cartoonists as Garry Trudeau see it. Since boys will be boys and girls will be girls, why all the fuss? It is at best another form of the fireworks attendant upon the celebration of "Liberty" in New York harbor. One makes whatever patterns his eye can make upon the star-bursts, even as they fade.

Meanwhile, one rests content in the pronouncement of the guru of Darwinian determinism, Edward O. Wilson: "I may be wrong, but I believe that the correct metaethic is the . . . fundamentally materialistic one. It works in the following way. Our profound impulses are rooted in a genetic heritage common to the entire species. These propensities are transmuted through culture into specific moral codes, which are integrated into religion and the sacralized memories of revolutions, conquests, and other historical events by which cultures secure their survival." One may, if he choose, from this position take "religious behavior very seriously as a key part of human nature." In this view one is safe, since "Metaethics can be tested empirically," as in the biological justification of condemning incest. Though Professor Wilson is Frank B. Baird, Jr., Professor of Science and Curator in Entomology at the Museum of Comparative Zoology at Harvard University, we have quoted him sufficiently to reveal him no logician or metaphysician. His "On

Genetic Determinism and Morality"[2] is a fossilized specimen of nineteenth century mechanistic determinism, spray-painted with the mystical glitter of twentieth century genetics. It is an idol comforting to one's feelings if not one's thought. Not to worry! Whatever will be will be. The war over pornography itself is but one of the events in biological evolution, affecting at some level the genes in our progress toward biological fulfillment.

Except, of course, the public spirit has become restive, no longer able to deny, it would seem, feelings prompted by the *intellectus*. For when one looks with the *intellectus* and *ratio* in concert at the general gnostic position, he discovers, in Wilson's statement above for instance, a multitude of questions begged by Wilson's *ratio*. The shell game whereby a Wilson rejects "a narrow form of genetic determinism" involves the slight-of-hand substitution of a broad form of genetic determinism, so vague in its parameters as to buy considerable time for the gnostic determinist. Certain genes, we are told, "prescribe particular responses." Thus "final thought and response" is "the product of a complex interplay of genes and environment. Social behavior in human beings is the result of biologically based predispositions filtered and hammered into final shape by the particular cultures in which individuals are reared." *"Believe Me!"* cries this complex of nonsense. Meanwhile be assured, given such vague and amorphous rules to this "materialistic metaethic," that "The evidence favoring the evolutionary approach to moral reasoning is as follows. By mid-1985 no fewer than 3,577 human genes had been identified of which about 600 had been placed on one or another of the 23 pair of chromosomes." As the others are identified and placed, all will be made clear, so that a "materialistic metaethic" can be established as one desires by the manipulation of genes, given our continuing faith that genes are the cause of an organism's response to environment.

---

[2]*Chronicles*, August 1986.

To the extent that such genetic structuring is revealed, to the extent that "the sensory and nervous systems appear to have evolved by natural selection or some other purely natural process, the evolutionary interpretation [of ethics] will be supported." In the worst scenario of this unfolding mystery of the genes, in the event the interpretation is not supported, "the evolutionary interpretation will have to be abandoned and a transcendental explanation sought." But that is a remote possibility. If not genes, then "some other purely natural process" (how telling, that *purely*) will come to the rescue. Perhaps Wilson here establishes the ground for a last battle in the twilight of determinism; at that point we shall no doubt be told that our genes have genes and a faith in determinism once more rescued out of its desperations. But the question is not so much whether pornographic art is the direct cause of violent sexual acts, a deterministic argument the opponents are tempted to embrace, as whether society should consent to the moral decay of which pornography is symptomatic.

Meanwhile, however, one's experience of reality suggests the bankruptcy of this guruship of nineteenth century science. The disarray of society in response to the bankruptcy of gnostic intellect is given spectacle in the battle over an idea, pornography. It is, by one of the ironies of history, a passion play occurring simultaneously with our rededication to "Liberty," and one finds in it the same unrest, the same sense that sexual "festival" (pornography) is fundamentally inadequate for the same reasons that patriotic "festival" in the worship of liberty is inadequate. Both violate that love which one experiences when he is in tune with creation.

xii

I should like to underline this absence of love in pornography, a species of nihilistic hopelessness, by examining the response of the Feminists to the Attorney General's report. We need only mention in passing a presence in that report of a mind quite comfortably at home with what we earlier considered as a Puritan survival of ancient Gnosticism, a Fundamentalist Gnostic mind. The most curious coincidence, at first thought, is the alliance between some Feminists and Fundamentalists (their common enemy here the secular gnostic fundamentalist). *Time Magazine* speaks of it as "The Feminist Dilemma."[1] Indeed the antifeminist political right and Betty Friedan do make strange bedfellows, a relationship that forces each to examine its position more carefully, but most especially forces Feminism to re-examine its ground.

What is immediately apparent is that within the Feminist movement is a confusion which is not quite so apparent in what *Time* calls the "antifeminist right." One Feminist faction, strongly opposed to pornography, asserts pornography "a virulent propaganda against women. . . . It promotes a climate in which the ideology of rape is not only tolerated but encouraged."[2] Betty Friedan warns against "Protectionist attitudes" that "ultimately hurt women," presumably because it is the male who seems cast in the role of protecting the female. She adds: "As repulsive as pornography can be, the obsession with it is a dangerous diversion for the women's movement." Nan Hunter insists that "Sexual abuse is not caused by violent sexual movies any more

---

[1] *Time Magazine*, 21 July 1986.
[2] Susan Brownmiller, quoted by *Time Magazine*, 21 July 1986.

than war is caused by *Rambo*," a most painful admission to make from within the movement, given the convenience of *Rambo* as a cudgel to use on the Attorney General no less than on the Secretary of Defense and that Rambo of Rambos (as seen by the Garry Trudeau groupies), Ronald Reagan. As for the National Organization for Women (NOW), the issue is so confusingly complex that this group watches "the uneasy alliance of Women Against Pornography and right-wing groups" with wary eye, taking no stand for or against pornography. In all the confusing babble, one word is conspicuous by its absence, a word we have argued as central to the discomfiting of gnostic spirit, Love. It is the absence of this key to the rescue of personhood, the healing unity of which melds *ratio* and *intellectus* so that person becomes attuned to creation, that is missing from the radical movement we call Feminism. That movement I take to be more simply another sect of secular gnosticism.

The premise upon which radical Feminism is built is a confusion of personhood with sex — sometimes an unthoughtful confusion, sometimes a most deliberate one. In proportion to the end sought as paramount objective in the movement, namely power, the confusion is deliberate. The movement for a while found itself increasingly appealing to the dislocated and disoriented, serving as a pseudo-religion, combining as it does a rhetoric of Freudianism and Marxism. The old "enemy of the people" is the new "male chauvinist," more easily identified by the accidents of biology than was that old bourgeois enemy. Indeed, the old enemy had to be eradicated by wholesale, and so indiscriminate slaughter, as of the Kulaks in Russia in the 1930s and of the Cambodians in the 1970s. This new enemy, however, is more selectively identified, since he is conspicuous by his bodily form. He wears it more symbolically (from a certain Feminist position) than the Paris Jews wore the Star of David in Nazi days. Even so the fittest of these enemies of woman, in their attempt to survive, very quickly learned the art of camouflage, androgynous disguise of dress and hair style. The rhetorical appropriations of Freudianism and Marxism allow an emotional manipulation of confused souls, male and female creatures alike. Lacking intellectual integrity — that is, lacking adequately established philosophical grounds and so forced to depend on the pseudo-science of Darwinian biology and the pseudo-philosophies of Freudianism and Marxism — it has the force of a cult.

The power base of Feminism has proved more extensive than that accompanying the rise of "Black Power" in the 1950s and 1960s, of which it is an historical development. Hence it has been more effective politically in its drive for gnostic power. (One of its spin-offs is the respectability of Deconstruction in the academy, the Deconstructionist usually proving most strangely to be also a Freudian, Marxist, Feminist.) It could be politically effective in a confused age simply because of the raw material available: in this country there are more women than men, but many fewer blacks than whites. In addition, it commands many men, some of whom had rather wear NOW buttons than risk being called unpleasant names with fish-monger intonations. So the movement commands a considerable statistical leverage in social programs of political intent. The Feminist position is, by its ground in nature and history, appealing to the oppressed, whoever the oppressed may be (racial minorities, homosexuals, lesbians). It is appealing because at its surface it offers an immediately believable explanation for individual failure and emotional confusion. Its romantic aura is captivating, in large part because it gathers to it a selective determinism bearing the stamp of science, especially of the soft (or as some would have it, pseudo-) sciences like psychology and sociology. One is what he is because of external dictates; and one is cheered to discover that there are others out there like oneself who are that way for the same reason; one is then member of a body within a larger hostile body which gives the smaller body its definition. It is an elect body, with a Calvinistic climate attaching to its emotional stance so rigidly as to make argument all but impossible.

But *member, body,* and such metaphor as here used carries none of the resonances possible when membership in existence is understood in the light of love. The radical Feminist demands respect, but the indications are that she fears love. Pornography, mistaken as a species of love, is thus doubly intimidating. Thus we have woman's "flight from woman." We have used Karl Stern's phrase figuratively, though the action described is often made manifest in the actual encounters between men and women. The flight, we also said, is a gnostic flight from reality, in its secular guise a withdrawal from being, a withdrawal sometimes made violent in its destructions of being. That is why one might justly say that often the radical Feminist sees existence itself as a species of pornography, including her (his) own body. The root issue, once more, is that of an ordinate love of creation, including the particularity of person. That is what we lose sight of in the confused and maddening Feminist extreme, a flight from man. The irony of that flight as increasingly revealed in the actual circumstances of the new woman in society: in her flight, woman would become man. The cold rage for justice that smolders in Clytaemnestra has its manifestations in the present movement, as one may easily demonstrate by listening to the manner in which demands for the deconstruction of reality are made in the social and political arenas by radical Feminists.

In Feminism, then, there is its own specialized version of secular gnosticism, programmatically established in the academy no less than pressed in government circles to be made national policy. Naomi Munson, in an essay review of Florence Howe's *Myths of Coeducation: Selected Essays 1964-1983,* examines Miss Howe's attempted "Escape from Nature." She finds Howe, "one of the founding mothers . . . of the scholarly field known as Women's Studies," teaching women to seek and attempting herself to learn "self-love."[3] It ought not to be necessary to say

---

[3]In *New Perspectives: U.S. Commission on Civil Rights,* Summer 1985.

that this is hardly the sort of self-love enjoined by the Second Great Commandment. The denial of the reality of Feminism itself, says Miss Munson, is "the very essence of Miss Howe's teaching." From the self-love song of J. Alfred Prufrock, private in his mind, we have progressed to the "Self-Love Song of J.A. Prunella" made programmatic for the whole of society. In the same issue of *New Perspectives*, Michael Levin finds "Women's Studies, Ersatz Scholarship," outraging those "scholars" who have staked their academic careers on the movement. He suggests that "All that a modern American woman shares with the wife of a fifth century Chinese peasant [such are the inviting comparative studies in the new discipline], but with no American man, are those biologically-based traits and experiences that feminists minimize or deny."

The academic climate surrounding and maintaining this species of "ersatz scholarship" is very like that supporting Deconstruction or neo-Darwinian determinism or deterministic sociology. Except that in the case of Women's Studies, reason is intimidated by a male sense of guilt (transferred upon reluctant females in some instances). One does not wish to appear "unjust," the sense of justness implied by such thought actually being a requirement that judgment of any sort absent itself. To be "unjust" in this murky sense is a more fearful condition than even appearing anti-intellectual, as in a philosophical opposition to Deconstruction. The consequences of this mythical and occultist Feminism within the academy is the elevation of the seminar topic, for which there is academic justification, into a degree program. To adapt what Father Jaki says in speaking of the Darwinian "humanism," Feminism in the academy is anti-humanist though asserting itself otherwise. In the Darwinian humanist form "brotherly love is evoked through despiritualized labels such as [for the Darwinian determinist] 'kin-selection;' and 'altruism,' lest the unwary be alerted to the fact that beneath the Darwinian guise of humanness there lurks 'scientific materialism as the best myth humankind may ever have.'" In Feminism's terms, such a label is the devil-term "role-model" to be converted to neutral. As with the term *life-style*, *role-model* implies that one is given being by dress and actions, a girl made girl by playing with dolls, a boy made boy by carpenter sets. Intrinsic reality, even at the level of Levin's "biologically-based traits" is denied on the authority of environmental determinism, but in the face of biological reality.

As Father Jaki observes, such pretensions to intellectual authority, however hollow, are welcomed by the academy: "nothing pleases nowadays more than academic respectability even if it is a cover-up for committing one big mental robbery through uncounted petty thefts — all of which are made imperceptible by phrases hollow inside their learned exteriors." Thus academic administrations on the one hand and mental burglars on the other establish a collusion, like that between Chaucer's apothecary and his physician: "For each of hem made other for to winne." The efforts are regularly in the news, sometimes playfully presented, as in this item from an evening paper: "Writers and Writeresses Can Avoid Sexist Language."[4] The attempt which is playfully reported is itself deadly seriousness, with academic sanction. The Project on the Status and Education of Women, a project of the Association of American Colleges, has published a "Guide to Nonsexist Language." It promises that "Breaking away from sexist language and traditional patterns can refresh your style." Never mind the presumptuous friendliness, the personal address ("your") to a vague audience: what is understood by *style* is the depressing presence. Now ships are to go on a *premiere*, not a *maiden*, voyage; there is to be no mention of "Founding Fathers," but we are to speak of them as *pioneers, colonists, patriots*. The *craftsman* is to be *craftsperson*. The dead ear of such guardians of our "style" is depressing. One wonders how these guardians can have been so careless as to overlook the *men* in *Women*, a part of its official

---

[4]*The Atlanta Journal*, 4 August 1986.

title, especially given its resolute rejection of *weatherman* in favor of *weather reporter* or *meteorologist*. When nonsense must be seriously met, as it must be here, we are in serious trouble, but none are more seriously troubled than women themselves.

Michael Levin engages the problem of Feminism in its social effects, suggesting that the movement is now at "Stage Three." This, he argues, is a historical turn "away from the goal of transforming women into pseudo-men and toward a new appreciation of motherhood and children." In his conclusion to an examination of radical Feminism's effect upon the fabric of society, which seems to be forcing the movement toward the ground of reality (compare the confusions within the ranks over pornography), Levin says, "The female as currently conceived by radical feminism is literally too good to be true, possessed of female needs superimposed on male aspirations."[5] What is being discovered within the movement, forcing reconsiderations, is the failure of this attempt at a gnostic alchemy, differing from that earlier pseudo-science in that — where the older alchemy attempted to turn base metal into precious — this new alchemy of Feminism attempts in its blindness to turn precious nature into a perverted nature.

At the level of biological transformation, Scandinavian surgeons have done sex-change operations, to the general solemn titillation of the media. But that is to operate at the surface of nature, not at those depths of the mystery of being wherein creation, including the particularity of person, is infused and infolded by Love. The gnostic self-love, inevitably a species of hopelessness, the presumptuousness of self-fulfillment through acts of the will, stands refuted by that encounter. But in the issue there is, dare we say it, a Feminist Fundamentalism which is slowly forced to the proximity of the Puritan Fundamentalist and into an uneasy alliance. Observing the coincidence of the two, as we observed of the Puritan Fundamentalist taken separately, one

---

[5]*Commentary*, August 1986.

is tempted to fierceness in condemning the spiritual alchemy attempted on the self. It is preached as a "born-again" religion by radical Feminism. One's anger stems from a realization of the vulnerability of persons, many of whom happen to be women by the gifts of nature, who are lured by ideological manipulations of nature to embrace and worship images of a spiritual millennialism: The Day of Woman dawning just over the horizon. In this millennial image, gnostic power would reshape woman to its own decreed pattern.

That pattern in Levin's words: "the best female life is taken to revolve around a fulfilling job [the job as substitute for beatitude, the *status comprehensoris*], paid maternity leave, then back to the 9-to-5 challenge." The wife is to be secure in the knowledge that her child is being cared for by a licensed, federally-inspected caregiver, the institutionalized Mother. That is, cared for by the "New Mother," in a Nominalistic slight-of-word intended to still the natural mother's disquiet. Science can do it better than she. But an older fundamentalism is not to be denied, those fundamental gifts in nature, a part of which is the being she actually is — namely, woman. Alchemy that would make her an ersatz man collapses, the new "role-model" blown outward from her roots of being, if she does not collapse first under the pressures of the ersatz-being imposed from without. Self-love is no match against the grace of being, with its intrinsic presence of Love. It can succeed only in creating a vacuum self. When a woman discovers that vacuum — and man has his own constructed vacuums of course, lest I appear to give a one-sided, chauvinist account — but when a woman discovers that vacuum in herself, it seems easy to slide into that other species of hopelessness, the presumption of the emptiness of all being, the climate of a nihilistic anticipation of fulfillment in nothingness. That is the wounded spiritual condition of woman that we are most likely to find ourselves confronted by in the 1990s as consequence of the Feminist Fundamentalism of the 1980s. And we shall especially discover it in those women who now devote themselves to Feminism as an academic discipline, assuming only that some residual intellectual curiosity lingers in the academy itself. Increasingly in this decade the woman executive is troubled by the disparity between her presumption of fulfillment as a "born-again" woman and her dream of the "job" as the millennial end. Perhaps the academic feminist, observing the plight of her sister in the world, may recover something of a balance from the *intellectus* to her severe perversions of the *ratio*. Meanwhile, by its serene, unvarying, abiding steadfastness, being — the reality of existence — devastates presumptuous thought, supplying the means to a recovery from the presumptuous inclination to despair.

We need not await the triumph of being over gnostic attempts at its deconstruction, since such deconstruction is a constant in human history. But neither may we stand aside on the ground that since the gnostic spirit is never eradicated the opposition is hopeless. The opposition is never hopeless in relation to one's own spirit and, in that most fundamental arena of spirit, the individual soul. Indeed quite possibly it may prove triumphant. That is the promise of hope. Meanwhile, we are called to action on being's behalf, since we are stewards of creation. One of those actions necessary is the exposing of weaknesses in the gnostic position. We must attempt just judgment of the truth of things, though we appear "unjust" to bankrupt gnostic thought.

xiii

What is one to do when confronted by the *ratio's* presence
as itself a product of animal evolution firmly anchored in the
physical brain no less than is the *intellectus* or "instinct"? Such is
one question spoken from within the gnostic's closed world, a
world increasingly intruded upon by being. Our latest science
makes it a probable question, if one's tacit view of existence is
that man is determined accident. One may not maintain a
hovering detachment from being by the *ratio* if it, too, evolves out
of animal body. That were a species of untenable superstition
because any transcendent cause of existence is denied in the
ground of the determinist's argument. One may act as if
independent, and the determinist in any of his manifestations
acts so — that is, acts as if his consciousness is quite separate
from all else. But he quite insistently declares all else
determined. Freudianism explains everything but Freud. Jung's
famous falling out with Freud was on exactly this point, Freud's
refusal to submit to analysis himself, as if God were required to
justify His existence to the creatures he created. Father Jaki
makes the same point in relation to Darwin: "Not once did he
ask himself the question whether his lifelong and most
purposeful commitment to the purpose of proving that there
were no purposes was not a slap in his mental face."[1]

Such works as Julian Jaynes' *The Origin of Consciousness in
the Breakdown of the Bicameral Mind* or the conference of equal
status of the "instinct" to reason in Betty Edward's *Drawing on the
Right Side of the Brain* puts both reason and consciousness in

---

[1]*Chronicles*, August 1986.

thrall to biological determinism. One may not put instinctive thought as a primitive residue, explained by that naturalistic determinism, to be manipulated by the rational mind on the authority of its presumption of a transcendence of nature, and at the same time reject the accompanying disclosures by the same science that consciousness has like origin and is itself anchored in the same primitive origins and beyond its own power to cut the cord that binds it to primitive animal nature. But the higher "instinct" that will not let one accept the contradiction, that forces one to engage prospects of order and proportion and meaning in a quest for the "truth of things," is a saving presence in consciousness, even when it has followed far along the road to its own gnostic dislocations. The disturbed modern consciousness is more and more forced to confront its failure to practice a significant alchemy on being. Father Jaki's words then have a special sting: "The aura that has grown around the modern word *evolution* is precisely the make-believe that something, and often something big, can ultimately come out from somewhere where it had not been before, provided the steps of the process are very numerous and practically undetectable." The God that is man when forced to admit itself only a spume of nature is caught in the throes of despair. Having insisted (in its modernist version) upon a premise of an unquestioned primal soup, out of which the accident called man develops, neo-Darwinism finds itself forced to examine its primal assumption, that uncaused cause, the primal soup. Confronted by that necessity, Darwinism is required to conclude itself, not science, but a poetic vision bordering upon metaphysics. Meanwhile, the relentless examination of being, centering in biology — in physiology and biochemistry — reduces the troubled consciousness to neural throb. Consciousness then begins to react with agonies like those the doomed fetus goes through with the intrusion of a saline solution into its once inviolable world.

Emerson's old insistences appear very quaint and unprogressive in these new circumstances: "Nothing is at last sacred but the integrity of our own mind." For Emerson, decidedly a modern gnostic, the identity of mind as the "ME" (his capital letters) leaves all else merely "apparition," including "all other men and my own body." Under the threat of a new conclusion by the rigid sciences of body and brain, consciousness is threatened with a conclusion that it is an effect of body, the body precedent in authority. Thus mind appears not so much a flowering beyond body as the determinist myth dreamed, but a faint glow out of genes, to be manipulated in the way one used to run up the old coal oil lamp wick. It is fueled by a primal stew of genes. The light of mind depends fatally, then, upon the burning genes. In every instance, that is save in that of the projector of the new metaphysics here described, the one whose hand is on the lamp stem. As always, mind as adjusted through mechanics can be used by this gnostic in his ravening of being; he alone is exempt from the deterministic pattern, is above it and so empowered to use it. One well observes, lest the point be lost, that mind so conceived is not mind, anymore than the word of Double-speak is either the idea it pretends or the thing from which idea depends. Neural response can be managed, as when an electrode is touched to a fresh frog leg. But the resulting action is not frog action. It is only a gnostic allegory of action from which the anagogic dimension of being has been excluded. A severed leg does not hop, though its movements may be harnessed in certain ways.

We are entering a period in the history of mind in which metaphysical questions are once more insistent, out of a growing panic in gnostic quarters. Only at the level of mechanical adaptation, at the level of technological innovations, does one still find a general obliviousness to metaphysical questions. For the most part, we are very nearly at a point where neither "objective" science (as opposed to its subordinate technologies) nor "subjective" humanism (as opposed to the specialized, isolated, and subordinate provinces of "humanism" such as Feminism, Deconstruction, or Freudian psychology) are any longer willing to accept mind as an effect of mechanistic existence. This is so even when *idea* yet glows with an old glamor of evolutionary theory, as in Professor Wilson's fatuous argument for a "materialistic metaethics." However, the trickle-down effect of earlier mechanistic theory yet forms our social, political, and religious thought in destructive ways, the Lucynell Crater Factor. A residual popular acceptance of determinism fuels the advertising industry, for instance, whether geared to sell soap or candidates. The technology that was an immediate consequence of the new religion of determinism yet builds paradises of sorts — air conditioned rooms within which one consumes improved beefsteak and liquor aged quickly in a detachment from time. The delight in modern "conveniences" will yet awhile sustain the myth, especially inasmuch as our weak sense of history does not remind us that the Industrial Revolution precedes Darwin and that Darwin is more nearly its effect than modern technology the effect of the Darwinian Science.

But modern gnosticism, the dominant religion since the Renaissance (whose priesthood is the intelligentsia), no longer finds itself comfortably leading a race to earthly paradise, to some divine secular city. We recall G.K. Chesterton's remark that to the medieval mind, life was a dance; to the Renaissance and post-Renaissance mind, it becomes a race. In the Age of Alienation, life is neither dance nor race, but an aimless scurrying under thickening and darkening clouds. It is to this moment of chaos that we have been summoning the monk and poet, the vision of a Thomas Aquinas and a Flannery O'Connor. For a considerable rescue from the dilemmas of consciousness in relation to being is there promised, a promise that may be tested by each person in the immediate concrete circumstances of his own particular existence, empirically tested in a way Edward Wilson does not admit in his quest for deterministic metaethics.

St. Thomas sees the *intellectus*, not as an instinct accountable to our animal natures, but as a visionary inclination in mind, a special gift to man's rational nature. He puts the observation thus:

> Although the knowledge which is most characteristic of the human soul occurs in the mode of the *ratio*, nevertheless there is in it a sort of participation in the simple knowledge which is proper to higher beings [angels], of whom it is therefore said that they possess the faculty of spiritual being.

Thomas is quite explicit elsewhere (in a passage cited several times by Flannery O'Connor) in asserting that the rational mode turns us toward nature as a first movement toward God. It turns us to encounter, through the body's senses, that which is neither the reaching mind nor limited by the body which particularizes that mind. We have suggested that the rational mind is drawn in this direction by the *intellectus*, a suggestion implicit in Miss O'Connor's saying that the reason goes wherever the imagination goes. She, too, is confident that in being thus drawn to an encounter with creation, we will have begun a journey to an encounter with the Cause of creation. In that encounter one discovers that "A higher paradox confounds emotion as well as reason," as she says to "A." That paradox arrests *ratio* and *intellectus* to their mutual dependence in the presence of the mystery of existence itself.

Thomas's argument is that the capacity for a participation through simple knowledge — intuitional or non-discursive knowledge, the "angelic" mode of thought — orients mind toward the transcendent. It "senses" the transcendent implications in creation. And this simple knowledge is "in" the *ratio*. It is that capacity in us that prompts us to speak confidently of knowing a truth "in our bones" or "in our blood." In this light, the relationship of *ratio* and *intellectus* is reversed from gnostic principles, whether those of the Puritan or the secular gnostic — both of which positions would have intellect ascend to beatitude by bypassing creation's complexity. The secular gnostic's version of transcendence is a sort of hovering above creation in the

manner of Edgar Allen Poe's "Earth Angels" or Rilke's "angels."
Between these imagined states of mind hovering over nature and
Emersonian "transcendentalism" centered in Emerson's "ME"
there is more than a coincidental relation. For in both, that
visionary recognition of the complexity of existence is rejected,
and in the rejection creation itself vaporized by the rational mind
through a Nominalist division of mind from creation.

Such, then, is the "trouble with you innerleckchuls," as
Onnie Jay Holy complains to that home-grown gnostic, Haze
Motes, who names non-existence as a last desperate defense
against both being and the presence of Love that alone makes
being substantial. Insofar as Flannery O'Connor is herself anti-
intellectual, she is so in that she stands resolutely opposed to the
separations and simplifications of existence by the gnostic mind.
Her "intellectuals" like Asbury or Rayber or Hulga, possessed of
"what passes for an education in this day and time," are rather
pseudo-intellectuals. But they are so, not because they lack the
formal training of mind they might have gotten at Yale or
Harvard or the Sorbonne, but because, very much in the recent
tradition of Western intelligentsia and especially as established in
such institutions as those, they embrace a partial knowledge as
the whole of knowledge and with it elevate themselves — their
"minds" — over existence. They are our version of what
Solzhenitsyn, in *From Under the Rubble*, calls the "Smatterers" in
his own country. Miss O'Connor praises Hawthorne as poet — as
visionary (though lamenting certain weaknesses of
craftsmanship). She does so because Hawthorne recognizes the
gnostic weaknesses in both his Puritan fathers and his neighbor
Emerson. And Hawthorne anticipates the gnostic road that will
be taken by the new science when it erupts upon the world out of
Darwin's imaginative poem, *Origin of the Species*. Such stories as
"The Birth Mark" and "Rappaccini's Daughter" show the point.
He reflects on the origins of our dislocation from being under
Puritan pressures in "The Maypole of Merrymount" and "Young

Goodman Brown." He engages the disjuncture of *ratio* and *intellectus*, head and heart, in "Egotism, the Bosom Serpent." Flannery O'Connor is herself the visionary poet, affirming reason in relation to imaginative vision and exposing modern gnosticism's separations. Her own term for the gnostic reduction of being in the interest of egocentric power is *Manichean* — a reduction whereby "Judgment is separated from vision, nature from grace, and reason from imagination." She uses the term often in its theological sense, but she applies it as well to secularized manifestations. In "The Fiction Writer and His Country," she remarks certain Christian writers who are "unconsciously infected with the Manichean spirit of the times and suffer the much-discussed disjunction between sensibility and belief."[2] In "The Nature and Aim of Fiction" she says that a Manichean separation of spirit and matter is "also pretty much the modern spirit," meaning the dominant secular mind.[3] She suggests that "the average Catholic reader," could he be tracked down, "would be found to be more of a Manichean than the Church permits," himself having consented to the separation of grace from nature and gradually to the ramifications of that consent in his soul. In so consenting, for instance, he is able to recognize nature in literature (says Miss O'Connor) in only two forms: "the sentimental and the obscene."[4] Since the sixteenth century, she says in "Catholic Novelists," "we live in a world that . . . has been increasingly dominated by secular thought." In consequence, the contemporary author and his characters "seldom now go out to explore and penetrate a world in which the sacred is reflected."[5] This popular spirit has embraced a new faith, tending more and more to believe "that the ills and mysteries of life will eventually fall before the scientific advances

---

[2]"The Fiction Writer and His Country," *Mystery and Manners*, p. 33.
[3]"The Nature and Aim of Fiction," *Mystery and Manners*, p. 68.
[4]"The Church and the Fiction Writer," *Mystery and Manners*, p. 147.
[5]"Novelist and Believer," *Mystery and Manners*, p. 158.

of men, a belief still going strong even though this is the first generation to face total extinction because of these advances."[6]

If popular gnostic belief denies to nature a participation in the mystery of existence whereby nature reflects the sacred, Miss O'Connor dramatizes that mystery. Her protagonists would use nature as an instrument against the threat of grace, denying nature's agency in mediating grace to man. Asbury[7] would usurp God's providence of grace through a sentimental communion with the milking parlor workmen, his milk of kindness hardly an adequate substitute for Christ's blood of sacrifice. It is appropriate dramatically that Asbury's come-uppance be through so unspectacular a medium of grace as a water-stain on his bedroom ceiling. The vision that is granted him is that he will continue to live in nature, for awhile, rather than quitting on his own terms, through his own romantic version of self-sacrifice. Similarly, nature becomes the tool which Mrs. May or Mrs. Turpin would use against the threatening presence of the sacred in nature. Their attempt to sterilize an arena — a pasture or the most modern pig parlor — fails, the relentless Reminder of the sacred invading their clearings to reassert the complexity of existence, to insist that (in St. Basil's words) there is always an "irrational residue" when finite rationality has done its best or its damnedest with being. Pigs glow with being. A rogue bull puts an inescapable point to Mrs. May in a most excruciating way.

For Flannery O'Connor, the long history of the "dissociation of sensibility," stretching back to the ancient Gnostics and Manicheans through separations of the *ratio* and *intellectus*, is apparent in the inadequate response of modernism to the nature of reality itself. Her refutation is in a dramatized confrontation of the gnostic by a grace denied. Anyone tempted to declare her anti-intellectual must first deal with that long history of

---

[6]"Some Aspects of the Grotesque in Southern Fiction," *Mystery and Manners*, p. 41.

[7]Flannery O'Connor, *The Complete Stories* (New York: Farrar, Straus and Giroux, 1971), pp. 357-382.

gnosticism and establish it as viable in the affairs of man as man deals with nature and his fellows. She herself understands the "pride of intellect" as it operates upon the popular spirit, and she knows at what key points it intrudes heavily in Western history. For she has a more considerable education in philosophy and theology than taught her, or most of us, in the schools. In her formal education, as she says, she received "what passes for an education." To put our conclusion another way, Flannery O'Connor's knowledge is such that one must also demonstrate as anti-intellectual those minds in concert with hers, those who share a view of modernism as intellectually flawed: Eric Voegelin, Hans Jonas, Jacques Maritain, Richard Weaver, Gerhart Niemeyer, Stanley L. Jaki, Etienne Gilson, Josef Pieper, Thomas Aquinas — a company of formidable minds of which hers is one. Till such work is accomplished, we must insist that at this present intersection of the past and future in our own present, we are well advised to be most skeptical of our intellectual guides, since they are for the most part secular gnostics. In the 1980s, they stand in baffled cohfusion, some of them slowly realizing that a light shines both on and from within the crossroads. It is toward this light that we need most to orient ourselves, if we are to be realists. That is, if we are to come to terms with "the truth of things" in such a way that we become also realists of distances.